October 1952

Ernest Walker

ERNEST WALKER
Drawing by Francis Dodd, 1934

Ernest Walker

BY

MARGARET DENEKE

GEOFFREY CUMBERLEGE

OXFORD UNIVERSITY PRESS

LONDON   NEW YORK   TORONTO

1951

Oxford University Press, Amen House, London E.C. 4

GLASGOW NEW YORK TORONTO MELBOURNE WELLINGTON
BOMBAY CALCUTTA MADRAS CAPE TOWN

Geoffrey Cumberlege, Publisher to the University

PRINTED IN GREAT BRITAIN

Preface

THIS book is the outcome of friendship. It may be said that it has grown and not been written. Left to himself Ernest Walker would never have told the story of his life; pencil games played in holidays formed the background for the first outline and in the last years the discovery of early diaries marked 'to be destroyed unread' gave him, my sister, and me pleasure and drew from his reticence further memories. The perspective of the story is influenced by what I had collected. His friend Dr. Cyril Bailey has gone over the manuscript with me and helped in the arrangement of the book. My sister has given me her assistance from first to last. To both of them I am sincerely grateful. To other friends of Ernest Walker thanks are due, especially to Dr. Ivor Keys who read all his compositions and added a chapter, and to Miss Alice Hess for two illustrations. I also have to thank the Fellows of Balliol College for permission to reproduce Francis Dodd's drawing and the *Oxford Times* for the photograph with Ravel.

MARGARET DENEKE

OXFORD
November 1949

Contents

Illustrations

1. Early Days

IN these days of specialization, even within the limits of a single profession, it is rare to find men or women who combine, as their fathers and grandfathers did, several sides or aspects of the whole. To this limitation Ernest Walker was a notable exception. As a composer he ranked high among his generation, especially for his songs; his *History of Music in England* has become a classic and his reviews and analytical notes always commanded attention. He was frequently heard as a pianist in Oxford, London, and elsewhere, and held a unique reputation as an accompanist. He was, moreover, a widely read man with a special love of poetry, and a thinker who had worked out his own philosophy of life. And behind all this lay a character of singular beauty, rigid in its integrity, deep in its sympathy, and incurably modest.

Walker's life was spent almost entirely in Oxford, and to Oxford music he devoted himself with a never-flagging zeal. In the period in which he lived there, something like a revolution occurred in the whole attitude to art. It was not merely that great music was far more often heard there, and large numbers of men and women in their time came to love and to make it. But from being a hardly tolerated adjunct to University life, it became recognized as an essential study and found its place among the Faculties. The standard of degree work was greatly raised, teaching was organized and made thorough, and the whole study lifted on to a higher plane. There were many, both professional and amateur, who took their part in this movement, but it owed more than can be measured to Ernest Walker. His self-effacement disguised this, but his own work as teacher and examiner did much to bring about the reforms, and the influence of the Balliol Concerts under his direction has affected the taste of many generations and given them something of that reasoned passion for truth and beauty which was the mainspring of his life.

It is the purpose of these pages to record the development of Ernest Walker's mind and character and to give some picture of his work.

Ernest started off on the longest journey he ever took before he was six months old. His father had held a post in the firm of East India Merchants, Lyon Lord, and had been engaged to Caroline Cooper for six years before the firm offered the partnership which enabled him to marry and take his wife to India in 1868. On 15 July 1870 Ernest was born at Bombay, and early in 1871 his parents brought him home to England to live with his maternal grandmother, Mrs. Cooper, and her daughter Emily at Bowdon in Cheshire.

Here he had a happy childhood and developed some of the interests and characteristics which remained with him through life. His care for animals is illustrated by the story that at the age of three he was found nursing a dead worm, indignant that it had been hurt. His daily walks, too, which he vividly remembered, may have laid the foundation of the mystic attraction that Nature had for him, as he pottered about among the dead leaves in Dunham Park, or enjoyed the adventure of plunging through bracken as tall as himself, whilst his nurse sat on a circular seat doing needle-work. Near at home, too, lay the Ashley water-mill, with the little River Bollin, about a foot deep, slowly winding its way through the meadows among flowers and bright stones, and now and then revealing a fish. The Bollin seemed so wide to the small boy—and when Ernest revisited it thirty years later it seemed so narrow.

The Charlesworth children from over the road provided companionship for bowling hoops or swinging on gates, and their small, handwritten 'Rose-hill Gazette' offered opportunities for help in copying out three neat columns under its printed heading and for putting into words strange bits of information. It is recorded that at four Ernest was reading a newspaper even before he had been taught the alphabet—a curious anticipation of the modern 'look and guess' method of teaching reading.

Music, too, had its place in these early years. In his grandmother's house there was an upright piano on which Ernest discovered that one could bang away with zest. And at Mrs. Hunt's school which he attended he had his first music lessons and learned to play the Diabelli duets, and not long afterwards solos, which were in request at friends' small parties.

In 1879 Edward Walker resigned his post with Lyon Lord in Bombay and accepted a position with the East India Merchants and Bankers, Forbes, Forbes and Co., in London. A suburban house was taken in Anerley, where the Walkers had the great satisfaction of being reunited and settling down together. The garden, her family, and her home were Mrs. Walker's world, for she seldom read anything, not even a newspaper, and her spare time was devoted to crochet work. Much of her interest was given to an entrancing little Skye terrier called 'Lulu', who for fifteen years lavished on her mistress her single-minded, warm-hearted devotion. She was a gentle little beast who shared a meal off her platter with a mouse nibbling at the other side. She refused the offer of a walk from anyone except her mistress; only on a Saturday would she consent to go out with the parlourmaid, because she knew it meant meeting her adored mistress coming home with her son from a piano lesson.

The father with his taciturn temperament and intense reserve was tied by the routine of a punctual and orderly City life. Every day except Sundays he caught the 8.15 train at Anerley, for he made a point of being at the office earlier than any of the clerks. When he returned after his day's work there would be a quiet meal followed by a silent evening spent in reading. In his study everything was in its appointed place; even inside the drawers each object lay exactly where it belonged and any sign of untidiness pained him. His bookcases were locked, but on a Sunday they would be opened and his son might choose a book for the day; it must be replaced in the evening till the next week. But under the monotonous outward calm there was in Edward Walker a deeply passionate nature, held in control by confiding his thoughts to a day-book or to sealed slips of paper all labelled 'to be destroyed unread'. He had published two novels under the name of Powys Oswyn, but his hope of a career as a writer had been buried with regrets before his marriage. After his return from India he gave up writing even short stories and his day-book became his only literary outlet.

Now and again, but at rare intervals, the settled routine of 226 Anerley Road would suffer upheaval by the giving of a dinner-party. The simple quiet life would be interrupted; sherry, port, claret, and champagne would be ordered, every domestic resource would be strained to the uttermost, the big chest with silver forks and spoons and dishes opened. The confectioner would deliver luscious pastries and the small Ernest tip-toed about to see all he could of the bustling preparations; he remembered how much he used to hope the guests would leave some of the dainties for him to taste the next day. A frequent guest was a faded, elderly, but alert Italian called Signor Boisragon, who had gone through the mysterious ritual of 'singing at Covent Garden' (Ernest always wondered what that meant). He would sing Rossini arias to his own accompaniment after dinner, or would pour praises on Ernest's solos, calling him 'piccolo miracolo'. Once a year Lord Farquhar, senior member of Forbes, Forbes and Co., would invite the Walkers to lunch at his house and to the pantomime afterwards. Ernest found the long-drawn-out meal hard to bear, for on each occasion it meant that they missed the beginning of the play. Once a year a gift of venison came from the Duke of Fife, who also had some vague connexion with the firm. The venison was usually too gamey for the Walkers to enjoy it, but its regular annual arrival always left a hope that next year it might be edible, whilst friends were only too glad to carry it off.

The move to Anerley changed life's horizon for Ernest.

No longer a big boy at Mrs. Hunt's little Bowdon School, he now became a junior at Mr. Serres's Penalvern School for Boys. But the really great gain was the nearness of the Crystal Palace. Here was a compendium of interesting information set out in life-sized models, a perfect paradise for a boy of his tastes. An old cousin of the Walkers remembered that Ernest had shown her round the Crystal Palace when he was nine. He knew the names and dates and whereabouts of everything and acted as a guide to classical and medieval statues, ancient temples, and stone antediluvian beasts in the lake; he was eager, too, to make her share his keen enjoyment of a cricket match or a concert. The days might pass in seeming monotony, but music and books lent a sense of adventure that coloured his existence. Isolation is a factor in life for most only children, and, as there was little chat in the family and hardly any talk about concerts or reading, Ernest dropped the more easily into the habit of thinking things out for himself and of confiding happenings to a small pocket-book.

At the age of twelve Ernest entered for the Junior examination of the Trinity College of Music in London and was awarded senior honours. About that time he was sent to South Norwood College, a private school of some twenty pupils whose headmaster, Mr. Bedford, was in appearance rather like the well-known picture of Chaucer. He was something of a scholar, and he gave to those of his pupils who could absorb it a good grounding in classics and a love of books. On Friday afternoons six or seven boys would be invited to his house, and Ernest would look forward to the spirited reading of Shakespeare in parts in the headmaster's private sanctum—a slightly awe-inspiring setting. Occasionally the whole school would read passages from the Bible, each boy taking his verse in turn. Mr. Bedford was a happy-go-lucky person, popular with his boys, and he had a gift for pulling off whatever he organized. Once Ernest saw him quivering with indignation: a boy's dog had bitten someone and had been condemned by the police to be destroyed. To save a vet's bill the father finished off the dog with a spade. Why Mr. Bedford should choose to tell a sensitive small boy about this ugly act of brutality seems hard to guess. But the fact that he was chosen by the headmaster for a confidence in white heat as well as the horribleness of it all weighed upon Ernest for days. It was the sequel to the worm at Bowdon.

There was considerable excitement at South Norwood College when Ernest, who was below the normal age to enter the Oxford Senior Locals Examination, came out in the class lists as the fifth highest in all England and the highest in music. The local press underlined the success. In those days all first-class candidates were given prizes; Ernest's was a pompously bound Milton.

Plans for Winchester College or Westminster were turned down on medical advice and Ernest stayed on at Mr. Bedford's school. But the splash in the Senior Local Examination had fostered a confident hope for Oxford and, if possible, Balliol, and when more advanced coaching in Greek and Latin prose seemed necessary, he was sent as a boarder to the Rectory at Writtle near Chelmsford. Here Mr. Papillon coached pupils for Oxford entrance. He was an ex-Fellow of New College commanding scholarship that

was finer than anything Ernest had met so far. His manifest
interest in the work with his new pupil proved stimulating,
and three months before he was seventeen Ernest was
accepted for admission to Balliol.

During his three months at Writtle his music looked
after itself. He composed half a dozen songs and snatched
some playing on the drawing-room piano when he could
get the room to himself. For the Writtle village concert he
set Byron's 'The Assyrian came down like a wolf on the
fold' and sang it to his own accompaniment with gratify-
ing success. For reasons of health the stay was cut short
and Ernest returned to Anerley, where he coached with
Mr. Bedford and F. H. Merk, senior scholar of Balliol,
whom Jowett had recommended. The first choice had been
Anthony Hope Hawkins, but he had accepted work elsewhere. Later in life Walker was much interested in 'Anthony
Hope's' novels, and it remained an amusing speculation
what kind of coach he might have been for a boy of
sixteen.

Ernest's father and mother were profoundly ignorant
about the qualifications of music-teachers, but their boy's
musical gift made them anxious to do their utmost for him.
Miss Robson was supplanted by Mme Krayn for piano
lessons, and Mr. Charles Cellier was approached for harmony. He was a brother of the composer of the popular
musical comedy 'Dorothy', a man with a decided streak of
vanity, and he enjoyed extending his patronage to a boy who
was beginning to make a name for himself locally. He invited Ernest, as the only juvenile performer, to play at his
Ballad Concerts—on one occasion the Op. 39 Waltzes by

Brahms and on others the six Novelettes of Schumann and the C sharp minor Impromptu of Chopin. Cellier foolishly instigated the publication of two pianoforte sketches that Ernest had dedicated to his mother. The proceeds were to go to the Norwood Cottage Hospital—needless to say there were none—and the fuss about his talent followed by critical remarks from his next more authoritative teacher gave Ernest a shock. Mr. Cellier should not have caused the boy to suffer this shame.

The Fine Arts Department of the Crystal Palace opened a School of Pianoforte Playing for Ladies, and Ernst Pauer, who had an appointment at the Royal College of Music, came from London once a week to give lessons to 'young ladies' in a large room on the first floor. The department was persuaded to forgive his sex and Ernest was admitted to lessons from Mr. Pauer. It was the first time he had encountered a musician of this calibre.

Pauer was a fine figure of a man, about six foot four and massive in proportion. He was in touch with the big world of music, but his teaching was casual and completely unsystematic. He would read *The Times* during part of the lesson whilst Ernest was scrambling through his *Gradus ad Parnassum* or pages of Hummel. Pauer took no trouble to cultivate a loose wrist or to think out fingering for his pupils, but he covered much ground and trusted that familiarity with the keyboard would bring command and nimbleness. It was something like a scandal that he added to his income by 'editing' the classics for Augener; the music was merely reprinted with a preface in bad English and a few poor woodcuts—yet Pauer liked his pupils to buy them. At any rate he put Ernest through much Beethoven, Mozart, and Schumann, a good many of the '48', and some Chopin. At every lesson he played with his pupil some of the classical symphony literature from the four-hand setting. Ernest learnt to rush from primo to secondo with only a bar to find his place on the page, and he enjoyed this practice of keeping one's head, and the pleasure of playing music already familiar in most cases from the Crystal Palace orchestral concerts. With a little more insight Pauer might have opened the door to classical chamber music by the same duet medium, but that world remained closed to Ernest till he got to Balliol.

Meanwhile, accompanied by his mother, he went to every orchestral concert at the Crystal Palace that could be fitted in with school routine—they saw a performance of 'Dorothy' and they attended Mr. Pauer's lectures, given in rasping English, illustrated by fine pianoforte renderings played by his son Max.

Pauer recommended harmony lessons by Alfred Richter, son of Friedrich Richter, Cantor of St. Thomas, Leipzig, who was in the direct tradition from Bach, just as Pauer himself through Hummel traced his musical descent from Mozart. Alfred Richter followed the Leipzig school of teaching, which was musically more flexible and intelligent than the Stainer-Ouseley creed that prevailed in those days. Ernest was doing double and triple counterpoint before he went to Balliol, but he had not attained that facility by the formal text-book methods.

Amongst happy recollections of early times many were connected with the Beaumont household. Captain Beaumont figured in the 1880s as a patron of music and chess. Ernest could recall distinctly the eager expectation with which the lonely boy would walk to that black house with red window-sills overhanging the London, Brighton, and South Coast Railway cutting; it meant much to him to meet others who made music. The ordinary routine was to call on a Sunday, to have tea and music, and if musically useful, one was asked for supper. Ernest often was. The setting was adequate: a fair-sized room, a conservatory attached to it where in a tank small alligators disported themselves—and an upright piano. One got used to the noise of the trains. Here Harold Bauer came with his violin—he was about two years younger than Ernest and the boys played together enthusiastically and often. Later on Ernest kept up these visits during Balliol vacations.

In a preface to J. D. M. Rorke's book *A Musical Pilgrim's Progress*, 1921, Ernest Walker describes his earliest musical memories:

'Peering into the mists that have gathered during the course of nearly half a century, I seem to discern, as the first objects of my whole-hearted musical affections, two grisly phantoms known respectively as a *Marche des Troubadours* by Henri Roubier and a *Gondellied* by Theodor Oesten; I have not been afflicted with a closer sight of either for years, but I have a vague impression, possibly unfounded, that the latter was slightly the less discreditable acquaintance, and a more definite impression that I loved the former rather the more ardently. No doubt I was a very small boy, but that is no comfort to me: I have known hosts of children of the same age who would scorn such low tastes. And the painful visions by no means cease there. I seem to remember, a little later, playing Beethoven's F sharp major Sonata and Thalberg's 'Home, Sweet Home' at one and the same concert (how appallingly I must have maltreated the former of this unholily yoked pair), and—quite certainly, I fear—wallowing in a new song about an Old Brigade (by one Odoardo Barri, if I recollect rightly) with extreme intensity of pleasure—I made a special point for a while of hearing the wretched thing whenever I could. And then came years during which I had, with queer indiscrimination, simultaneous enthusiasms for respectable and quite disrespectable things. I had what I know now to have been the inestimable advantage of steeping myself in the daily orchestral concerts at the Crystal Palace in August Manns's prime; but I must sorrowfully confess that an effusion called a Turkish Patrol, by one Michaelis—these details must have been deeply rooted to have stuck so vividly in my mind—that I often heard from the military band in the centre transept, gave me, for some time, at least as keen delight as anything I heard in the more select part of the Palace. Later, in my undergraduate days, I kept a more or less regular musical diary: most of its entries read fairly decently, but I know very well, though I never committed the fact to paper till now, that for a quite considerable while some of my crowning emotional ecstasies were infallibly evoked by Stainer's Sevenfold Amen. Mr. Rorke began with Chopin without any of these horrible strayings; but having now abased myself in the dust, let me try if I cannot get a little more even with him in recalling the more creditable features of my evolution.

There is an ancient Oxford story of an undergraduate who, being requested to specify the minor prophets, replied that it was not for him to make invidious distinctions among holy men; and similarly, in naming the great names, I am as far as Mr. Rorke is from any desire to draw up judicial class-lists. Roughly chronological landmarks, so far as I can recall them, were the fourteenth of Mendelssohn's 'Songs Without Words', Beethoven's C sharp minor Sonata and, very markedly but later, *Leonora No. 3* (I invariably choked at the climax of the coda), Chopin's G major *Nocturne*, the *Warum* of Schumann (a very powerful long-sustained influence), Schubert's

C major Symphony, the *Lohengrin* Prelude, the *Les Préludes* symphonic poem of Liszt (a merely meteoric force), and the *Liebestreu* and *Von ewiger Liebe* of Brahms, who appeared suddenly with a vehement attack. Of Bach I knew little, and that did not appeal much; at Mozart I rather sniffed. *Horresco referens.* It seems, perhaps, a queer hotch-potch of positives and negatives; but somehow I fancy I see a thread running through it all, a thread that, after many more twistings and turnings, I still hold in my hand unbroken.

Change is, I suppose, the law of music as well as of life; and we have to prove all things (and there are certainly plenty of them) before we can quite know how to hold fast that which is good. I whole-heartedly agree with Mr. Rorke about the greatness of *La Cathédrale engloutie*, but I recall as vividly as if it were a matter of yesterday my complete bewilderment when this new planet swam into my ken; there seemed to be nothing in my musical world with which to correlate it. But now it seems far more plain-sailing than some things which I have known twice as long. And so, when one's pupils bring compositions that appear at a first glance to read equally well upside down, one must not too hastily conclude that that is the last word to be said about them. Another generation is evolving in its turn; and, after all, it has escaped from the *Marche des Troubadours*.

2. Balliol 1887–1900

1. *Friends, occupations, and interests*

IT was a proud sense of achievement which the inexperi-
enced shy boy of seventeen felt when he installed his
belongings in a room at the top of staircase 22 adjoin-
ing the Hall. Balliol had been ardently hoped for, and
planned with much loving care by his father; and now
dreams had come true. The window of his room looked
out on the garden quad where a game of bowls was being played on the lawn, and gaunt elms hid the old wall
to St. Giles'.

Ernest's first outing was to Taphouse to hire a piano;
there was as yet no Steinway in the Hall. The senior scholar
of Balliol, G. C. Richards, called and laughed in a very
kindly way at the fresher who was overwhelmed at the distinction this visit seemed to confer. A friend describes
Ernest at that time as having 'a good face with very blue
eyes and an exceptionally spiritual expression'. Health was
improving, but at no time could physical nervousness be
altogether ignored, though in course of years it diminished.
However, Walker found his feet at once, and it speaks well
for Balliol that the undergraduates adopted their youngest
member with such friendliness.

Like most men in his day Walker was to take the full
Classical Honours course, and indeed his previous work
had prepared him for it. Honour Moderations he took in
1889 and obtained a second; more could hardly have been

expected with his rather sketchy background. His tutor was a brilliant young scholar, W. R. Hardie, afterwards Professor of Humanity at Edinburgh, and his work also brought him into contact with Francis de Paravicini and Evelyn Abbott. The Mods. curriculum is linguistic and literary, and it certainly enhanced Walker's love of literature and his sensitive ear for style and rhythm. There are notes of the reading of Greek and Latin books in later years, and it is remarkable that when in 1923 he undertook to write music for the performance of the *Rhesus* by the O.U.D.S. in New College garden his settings reproduced admirably the rhythm and feeling of the original. But it was not till he began his reading for Greats in the summer of 1889 that he really came into his own. The philosophy fully satisfied his desire for accurate thought and set his mind working on lines he never afterwards forsook. In this he was greatly stimulated and guided by his two philosophy tutors, R. L. Nettleship and Charles Warrack, of whom more must be said later. His work was regarded as very promising and hopes of a first class were held out. In an amusing letter to his parents on 24 June 1890 he describes his interview with the Master and Tutors at 'handshaking':

The Master said 'Some people say music and work don't go together, but I don't think that's the case with you, Mr. Walker. Your examination is very satisfactory indeed, and Mr. Abbott tells me your History paper was exceedingly good. If you keep your health, and work prudently, I certainly think you should get your first in a year's time. Don't you think so, Mr. Nettleship?'

Nettleship (quite taken aback, and obliged to say something), '—Oh yes, most certainly.'

The Master (resuming very graciously), 'We're very glad to have you here. Thank you for playing the organ. Goodbye.'

Although their hopes were disappointed and in July the next year Walker was placed in the second class, he was told by Strachan-Davidson that he was just on the line of a first and that the Senior Examiner (the Rev. W. A. Spooner, afterwards Warden of New College) voted strongly for it, but was overruled by his colleagues. Walker took his B.A. soon afterwards and proceeded to his M.A. in 1894.

To complete his academic record it must be added that as a graduate he wrote at Jowett's 'order' an essay on Erasmus for the Chancellor's Prize, and that in due course he took his degrees in music, B.Mus. in 1893 and the Doctorate in 1898. The college appointed him as assistant organist to Farmer in 1891; Jowett spoke of him as 'a musical don'. Nettleship and Hardie had misgivings and wrote to Edward Walker pointing out that Balliol had no sort of right to claim any sacrifice of his son's career. But Ernest felt he was fortunate to have the prospect of a permanent link with Oxford; he was eager to do what he could for his college, and in comparison with that the alternative of travel or musical study abroad scarcely weighed at all. The new position gave him a definite status and a reason for staying in Oxford.

This bare record must be supplemented by his own recollections and observations. His father presented him, when he went up to Balliol, with a diary, and from 1888 to 1894 he kept it fully, recording his friendships, his reading, his thoughts, and his experiences.

Walker's chief friends, whose names recur frequently,

As an undergraduate

As a boy with Lulu

JOHN FARMER

were E. J. Palmer ('Jimmy'), afterwards Fellow and Chaplain of Balliol and later Bishop of Bombay, and C. J. M. Gordon, afterwards Master of Kelvinside Academy, who died in 1921. With these two, when he went out of college in 1890, he lived in lodgings at 15 Ship Street. Bishop Palmer writes: 'We were a very happy partnership. All of us worked hard at our reading for Greats. My impression of Ernest in those days is that he was rather shy, but very pleasant to talk to, and he had various interests, such as young men have at the University.' Others whose names occur in the diaries are G. W. Hockley, the Blundell Scholar of the year, who later became Archdeacon of Cornwall, and F. M. Anderson, two years junior to himself, who died young in 1899. It was the habit of these friends to read books together and to discuss them either in undergraduate societies or among themselves. The diaries record these readings and discussions; they show how a new world of thought opened to Walker and suggest the general trend of his reflections. Some extracts on general literature may be quoted first.

18 OCTOBER 1890. Read *Leaves of Grass* to each other in evening: really although Whitman does extremely often write what can hardly be distinguished from obscure amusing nonsense, he sometimes rises to really grand rough strong outbursts and meditations that are very fine. And although the outspoken frankness of some parts is appalling, yet one cannot call the man immoral. The man has such wonderful faith in all Nature and the human body in particular that even his sometimes extremely unnecessary pieces of realism on sexuality don't sound wrong. The Devil could certainly quote Walt Whitman as well as the Bible for his own purposes: but so he could most books—in fact, all worth anything.

20 OCTOBER 1890. Gordon had a meeting of the Milton Club in his room in the evening, so I went in and listened to a paper and discussion on Renan's *Vie de Jésus*—all sorts of views, from the more or less orthodox Liberalism of the paper to more or less complete agreement with Renan—all well and forcibly expressed, but throughout studiously temperate.

My view of the book is that it is one of the most fascinating romances in existence: but it is terribly French in parts, and some things in it—such as the view of the raising of Lazarus—are ludicrous. But it contains some superb pieces of lofty noble writing; and as to its historical value—well, our materials are so extraordinarily obscure that, making somewhat copious allowances for Gallic aberrations, it perhaps gets rather nearer to the truth than most similar studies—and certainly infinitely nearer than the *Leben Jesu* of Strauss. But from some others of Renan's works one seems to get the impression that the spirituality of this book is but elegant writing, and that the man's real views are nearer that light-hearted cynicism—'les frivoles ont peut-être raison'—which is the very lowest depth that the human soul can reach.

14 NOVEMBER 1890. Read Swinburne at our usual after dinner reading. The man has no doubt written some fine things especially parts of *Atalanta in Calydon*: but the music of his verse is very far from approaching the bests parts of Keats and Shelley and still more of Spenser—while the majority of his poems are mere voluptuous pieces of lusciousness with no thought in them at all: and a more profoundly immoral poem than *Dolores* it would be hard to find. If I had a sister I would rather read her the whole of Walt Whitman unexpurgated a hundred times over than such a piece of serpentine sensuality once—and I would throw in all Catullus and Aristophanes along with Whitman.

23 JANUARY 1892. Finished Thomas Hardy's *Tess of the D'Urbervilles*. A really great book, I think, on the true tragic model; but terribly sad. All the wonderful country descriptions and lighter

scenes only throw into stronger relief the one central strain—'O the pity of it!', and the end leaves one with a sheer dull aching pain and feeling that 'He causeth his sun to shine on the just and on the unjust'. A book that is 'realistic' in the best sense—a plain picture of all sides of life, and the mingled humour and pathos of it all, and finally the mockery of this sorry scheme of things entire—that Fate is usually unjust rather than the opposite.

21 OCTOBER 1892. Walk beyond Headington in afternoon. Composed, as usual, at my Rhapsody, and reread *Sesame and Lilies*—in spite of all Ruskin's crankiness in the majority of his other books, one does feel somehow that there is something extraordinarily fine about the mixture of passion and tenderness with which he preaches the doctrines of the true spiritual life.

Two booklists entered in 1894 will give an idea of the range and variety of his reading.

8 MARCH 1894. Principal books read or reread last term: Horace Odes: Sappho and other early Greek Lyrics: Greek Anthology (Mackail's selections): Lamennais—*Paroles d'un Croyant*: Heine—*Reisebilder*: Merimée—*Carmen* etc.—*Lettres à une Inconnue*—*Dernières Nouvelles*: Tourgenieff—*Pères et Enfants*: W. Morris—*Poems by the Way*: Coleridge—*Table Talk* and *Human Essays*: Huxley—*Science and Education*: Guizot—*Histoire de la Civilisation*: Leslie Stephen—*Hours in a Library*: Scott—the *Antiquary*, *Waverley*, *The Bride of Lammermoor*: De Maupassant—*Boule de Suif*: Hawthorne—*The Scarlet Letter*.

18 JUNE 1894. Heine—*Deutschland* and all poems except *Buch der Lieder*: Goethe—*Wilhelm Meister*: Hatch—Hibbert Lectures on *Greek Influence on Christianity*: Meredith—*Rhoda Fleming*: Hardy—*Life's Little Ironies*: Renan—*Origines du Christianisme* (7 vols): Tacitus—*Annals, Germania, Agricola*: Pascal—*Pensées*: Yeats—*The Celtic Twilight*: Sophocles—*Oedipus Coloneus*: Terence—*Phormio* and *Eunuchus*.

There was little except science and mathematics that did not rouse his intellectual curiosity and claim his enthusiasm. He learnt now to tear the heart out of a book by use of an index, and to read at a great pace.

Balliol undergraduates at that time were not encouraged to attend lectures out of college, but after taking his degree Walker went to hear Walter Pater and made his personal acquaintance. The comments in the diary are characteristic.

21 OCTOBER 1891. Lecture at B.N.C. this afternoon by Walter Pater—the first of a series on 'Plato and Platonism'. Ostensibly on Heraclitus and leading up to a detailed exposition of the gospel according to Pater, largely taken word for word from the epilogue to the 'Renaissance'. An exceptionally brilliant lecture in Pater's own wonderful style; but in spite of the marvellous 'glamour' that such an individual sort of person manages to produce, one feels after the spell is off that after all a one-sided refined sensuality like that is hardly the whole of life. The worship of beauty is no doubt in itself a noble creed which in England especially wants enough enforcement; but when it leads to a face like Pater has now, one feels somehow that something has gone wrong with it. In spite of the marvellous beauty of his books, one feels that it is an atmosphere in which one can't breathe quite freely.

28 OCTOBER 1891. Second lecture by Pater—on the Eleatics—but as before, largely taken up with applying their principles to modern thought. Again a marvellously brilliant performance, and all the more suggestive from the fact that the man's whole conception of philosophy and his scorn of metaphysics is so very different from what one ordinarily hears.

4 NOVEMBER 1891. No Pater lecture. He has given up for some reason or other just like he did last term.

Pater invited any of his listeners to call on him at B.N.C. and Walker took him at his word.

Once he was Pater's guest at dinner at B.N.C. and several times at his private house: 64 St. Giles'. Here the table was spread with beautiful Venetian glass and both before and during dinner a huge blue Persian cat walked about on the table, threading her way among vases and tumblers without breaking anything. What seemed most odd to Walker was that no one worried about the cat's doings; she was completely ignored.

In 1893 Walker called and found Pater at work with a large bowl of dried rose-leaves on his writing-table. Walker observed that the lines of his page were very far apart, space being left to correct the swing of the rhythm and to get 'le mot juste'. Talk turned to Belgium, where Walker had been travelling: he spoke about the Rubens in Notre-Dame at Malines and Pater was interested that he had discovered for himself something of outstanding beauty off the beaten track. It was a painting for which Pater had a special liking. But when Pater spoke of music and waxed enthusiastic over Gounod and the Salvation Army Band, Walker sought refuge in silence.

One of Ernest Walker's most salient characteristics was his urge to attain mental clearness; his zest never allowed half-measures. The account of the discussion on Renan's *Vie de Jésus* shows that in his early undergraduate days this faculty was applied to questions of religion and theology. But in fact the process had begun before that. At fourteen he took confirmation seriously; indeed, so much so that it was a shock to him to see the curate play football immediately after the confirmation lessons. There was no reason why this should be incongruous, but a doubt flashed through Ernest's mind whether the solemnity he had just experienced had been as sincere and profound as he had supposed. A few years later, on a Good Friday, he was overwhelmed with the significance of that day in the world's history, and the holiday spirit of Brighton where he and his parents were staying jarred on him. He went for a long walk alone, dwelling intensely on his thoughts till he was overcome by a mood of exaltation that amounted to a definite religious experience.

The earliest diary (1888) is almost an index to the services of Holy Trinity, Anerley. Vaguely he contemplated taking orders, but that idea faded out. The interest in varieties of religion continued, and he felt compelled to face ultimate issues. Much of his reading was devoted to religious books; he grappled with most of Renan's works, Tolstoi's powerful and striking *My Religion*, Morley's *Compromise*, Lecky's *Rationalism*, and any number more, English, German, and French.

In the undergraduate years Hockley, already a convinced High Churchman, would discuss theological questions with Walker and with him sampled various religious services.

8 MAY 1889. 'Spent a long time in hunting the locale of the Jews' "Tabernacle" where Hockley and I think of going on Friday.'

Of St. Barnabas the diary reports:

'Really that High Church Ritual manages to appeal to one's aesthetic sensibilities in a remarkable degree, which makes it much less tedious than Evangelical services—though the two are about on a par in all other respects. Still nineteenth century Christianity robbed (however illogically) of its old cruel elements, is a marvellously beautiful thing—about the most lovely fairy-tale that ever grew up. But—"la vérité est toute pour tous". The childhood of man is beautiful but it has to pass.'

About the same time Hockley introduced Walker to Gore, who was then Principal of Pusey House.

A most charming man and one that one feels could be implicitly trusted, although one might not agree in his ritualistic views. Coffee and conversation generally, and Compline afterwards in the small chapel. He has a face which is like nothing so much as a mediaeval Christ.

Gore's first Bampton Lecture was a fine sober unrhetorical sort of sermon showing strongly his manly intellectual fearlessness and remarkable fair-mindedness, though I can't manage to be convinced by such arguments.

Later on Walker refers to *Lux Mundi*.

10 MAY 1890. Read *Review of Reviews* for May in which the place of honour is assigned to a synopsis and review of *Lux Mundi*. I have not read all these twelve essays yet, but as to the one of Gore's on Inspiration, which is the principal point of attack, I must say that I think his opponents have the stronger position. I cannot see any way of getting out of the fact that to deny Daniel and the Davidic authorship of the Psalm which Christ deliberately asserts, is implicitly denying the infallibility of the latter. And to talk about double nature etc. really lands one in the dilemma as to what utterances are to be put down to the human and what to the divine. We have no criterion except to say he has been proved wrong on some points and therefore that part of him is human. But it is surely dangerous to take that line. It would be impossible to contradict anybody who chose to say anything was wrong and human. Liddon is certainly right in saying that to a believer in the divinity of Christ all such questions are *ipso facto* foreclosed. But we ought to be

thankful that men in such a position as Gore have got *some* advanced views, even though they do not see they are standing on a precipice. The Reformation truly was, as Von Hartmann has said, 'the suicide of Christianity'. It emancipated men from one bondage, only for the time to cast them into another; but still the one act of emancipation has done its work. Little by little fragments have been dropping off—and now in *Lux Mundi* and all books of education, the old theory of 'plenary inspiration' is dead. It is seen that the Bible is no ultimate resort on all points, but when we once get there, I don't see what there is of dogmatic Christianity left.

A year or two later after he took his degree Walker refers again to a meeting with Gore:

16th FEBRUARY 1892. Lunch with Gore at Pusey House and a long walk with him afterwards. He is really an extremely fine sort of man, and with the keenest and most unconventional literary insight, as well as a strong sense of humour. Altogether I had a most delightful talk the whole time—on all sorts of subjects, frequently theological (Keim, Renan etc.). I had been rather afraid that he might 'examine' me a little which would have been uncomfortable, especially if he had put his arm round my neck, as he often did (it's his regular way)—but he never did so at all.

It is clear that Gore's influence was not likely to bring Walker back to orthodox Christianity, but the extracts are interesting in showing his appreciation of Gore's personality and his own fairness of mind.

Other extracts from the diaries illustrate the progress of his mind towards agnosticism and foreshadow the complete rationalism of his later years—but in all there is a sympathetic sensitiveness towards those with whom he could not agree:

21 JANUARY 1890. Read W. S. Lilly's *A Century of Revolution*

—a very comprehensive book, written with a very great deal of hard hitting. I don't know if his representations are always correct, but most unquestionably I think that the only salvation is to be found in the recognition of Idealism and the Spiritual as the one highest Reality. One must make one's 'act of faith'; and to me the predominance of the spiritual seems the necessary corollary from the first absolute hypothesis—the intelligibility of the world. 'Self-reverence, self-knowledge, self-control' is the eternal basis on which personal ethics must subsist: and it seems to me that to adopt modern Naturalism and Sensualism is simply to fly into the face of progress. When Paul Bert says that his main aim is to find something to destroy Christianity and all religion with it, the only conclusion one can come to is that the man is a most pernicious fool. Although theoretical Christianity may have embodied propositions which are now seen to be untenable—although its ethical system may originally, as on such a question as chivalry (about the most priceless Teutonic bequest), have been entirely inadequate, yet its cardinal spirit of Universal Love has sunk too deep into man to be ever eradicated now. A man is not reverenced as God for 1800 years for nothing: if anyone has conquered the world, it is the Carpenter of Nazareth.

6 MARCH 1890. Read Edwin Arnold's *Death—and Afterwards*. I think we must come to the conclusion that the only satisfactory basis for the hope of personal immortality is that 'healthy mysticism' of love and emotion. . . . But I really think the position we must take up is that expressed in these grand words of the often very unpleasant writer Sir J. F. Stephen—'Above all, let us dream no dreams, and tell no lies, but go our way wherever it may lead, with our eyes open and our heads erect. If death ends all, we cannot meet it better. If not, let us enter whatever may be the next scene like honest men, with no sophistry in our mouths and no masks on our faces.'

6 SEPTEMBER 1891. [At Amiens] A most pathetic notice, I thought, posted up in the Cathedral asking 20,000 working men of

France to pay a visit to Rome 'pour consoler le cœur de l'illustre prisonnier du Vatican . . . '. But still with all the pathos mixed with despicableness of this sort of thing, one feels that in a Cathedral like this or Rheims one gets very near the kernel of the Roman Catholic religion—outside all its vices, which are quite numerous enough, one feels that there is something eternal under it all, and I had no scruples in sprinkling myself with holy water in reverence of the men who, at any rate in stone, searched so splendidly after God.

5 AUGUST 1893. Read Coventry Patmore's *Religio Poetae*— a curious and rare type nowadays: pure mediaevalism—strong mysticism, essential inferiority of woman etc., but some striking bits of writing. Certainly I think with Patmore that Christianity in its earliest essence was infinitely more mystical than meditative, and more exclusive than philanthropical and practical. I don't suppose that its founder ever imagined it was meant to regenerate the world in general—the whole essence of it was that only a few would be capable of it. Its end was infinitely more contemplative union with God—in a word mysticism—than hospitals and things of that sort, which were pure excrescences. It has nothing, to all intents and purposes, whatever to do with the outside world, about which its founder, at any rate, did not concern himself—still less had it anything to do with arguments of any kind whatsoever.

10 NOVEMBER 1893. Been reading a good deal of Matthew Arnold again. One gets rather sick of his phrases and mannerisms, and though he deserves remarkable credit for seeing that Christianity means a good deal even when we disregard its dogmas, yet it is absurd to try and bridge over, as he does, the enormous gulf which must separate the sincere believer from the sincere disbeliever, who may yet appreciate to the fullest extent all the mysticism of Christianity and everything else in it. The gulf which separates the whole views of life of the two is incalculable.

In Walker's essay on Erasmus there was a good deal of himself, and his contrast of Erasmus and Luther with which the essay concludes reflects much of his own mind. A few sentences may be quoted:

The reformation of Erasmus might in the course of time have produced an intellectual atmosphere in which all superstition would have imperceptibly vanished; but would not the result rather have been that condition of spiritual life which some modern writers seem inclined to favour, in which all the intellect of the country looks on religious belief with a mild and kindly tolerance, as an excellent thing for the lower classes? The result of the Lutheran Reformation has no doubt been of a very mixed character, but it has not led to universal hypocritical compromise. Erasmus was fond of expressing his view that the truth about things was often better concealed from the multitude. We may admit as fully as Erasmus would have admitted that truth is in its essence many-sided, and that there is a truth of ideas as well as a truth of fact. Yet we know from the history of intellectual questions that the doctrine of concealment of truth has too often led, not to the inculcation of what is recognized as the same truth in another perhaps less true setting, but to the direct preaching of what is known to be false.

Oxford gave a great stimulus to Walker's love of nature, and as one reads the diaries, it is seen that the mystic attitude to nature, which was shown even in childhood and is exhibited in many of his songs, was becoming a stronger and stronger element in his life.

About sixty years ago Oxford was still surrounded with open country; the roads were quiet and fields and copses were only a mile and a half from Carfax. To one as acutely sensitive to moods in nature as Walker they proved a living experience.

One of the most frequent entries in the diaries is 'worked and walked as usual'. Walks as a rule might be six or eight

miles; as an exception they would extend to Woodstock or
Dorchester; all the villages round Oxford are mentioned in
turn: 'Powder Hill copse all blazing with bluebells',
'Binsey in October glowing in red and yellow'. An afternoon 'to Garsington and back', and an evening 'to Mar-
ston Woods to hear Nightingales . . . woods are the place
for thinking'. Or 'sat down by a stream near Hinksey and
investigated the habits of frogs and water-beetles for over
an hour'.

30 OCTOBER 1891. Walk to Wytham in the afternoon—a
glorious day—a cloudless sky and a sort of constant soft Corot-like
sunlight all over. And those woods! Really the whole scenery round
by them, village and all, is practically perfection in its style—and
surely the worship of shades of green is an element in the highest
life.

30 MARCH 1892. A superb spring day, so spent the morning on
Cumnor Hurst where I took some music paper and worked. What
supernatural beauties of colouring one can see in ploughed fields
with the sun on them. I nearly go mad sometimes with the beauty
of all nature in which there is nothing common or unclean.

31 MARCH 1892. Worked all morning in the fork of a pollard
willow by the Ferry Hinksey backwater . . . lay down in the grass
and lost myself for three-quarters of an hour or so in watching
weeds grow a flaming gold in the sunlight and listening to the breezes
whispering along the hillside. 'There is a great God in them who
does not grow old.'

23 OCTOBER 1892. A splendid clear soft light and that view over
Wood Eaton from Elsfield Hill was certainly today one of the most
wonderful things I have ever seen. Fletcher, who has a strong nature
sense (certainly a sense wanting in most people up here, I think,
though most of my intimate friends have had it), was quite wild over

it, and we both got a strange feeling which does come over one when one stands watching the play of light and shade on birch leaves as they flutter off the tree.

There are also detailed accounts of 'outings in Jimmy's beautiful Canadian canoe' and records of holiday tours. One holiday spent on a walking tour in Scotland with his friend Gordon in 1890 lights up the pages of the diaries with glowing descriptions of twenty-mile walks in the Highlands; and superlative enjoyment is again recorded in 1891 when he first visited Switzerland with the Farmer family. It was on this holiday that he grew the beard which, brown at first and later a silvery grey, was so conspicuous a feature to all his friends.

During those early post-graduate years Walker composed many of his songs—sometimes they flowed freely, six in two days on one occasion. He chose nature-poems, sometimes from Rückert and Uhland, when he wrote the English versions himself. Both these translations and his settings show the intensity of his feeling for nature.

II. *A Trio of Dons*

It has been seen that even before Walker came up to Balliol, the Master (Benjamin Jowett) had shown great interest in him; as soon as he was in residence at Balliol a personal relation between them was firmly established, and Walker's diaries (1889–94) show how much he was one of the Master's boys. There is mention of 'walks alone with the Master' and 'talks and breakfasts with no-one else' and evenings of 'solitary' conversation when all the talking fell to Walker. There are requests for music for the

Master's guests and invitations for dinner, or wine. It was always an event to be asked to share dessert and half an hour's good talk with the Master's week-end party before they rejoined the ladies. These dining-room scenes were impressive, and the French butler Perroud added to their solemn dignity. On one occasion, when Walker took the seat of a guest who was compelled to leave, the Master quoted Virgil's 'primo avulso non deficit alter aureus'.

On a Sunday evening the Master liked to take his party to the Balliol Concerts, and his entry was a great moment. Jowett used to troop in with a galaxy of distinguished guests, the audience rising to its feet as he walked the whole length of the Hall: Huxley, Lord Coleridge, Browning, Tennyson, Arthur Balfour, Margot Asquith, Mrs. Humphry Ward, and many others were among them. Andrew Lang has left on record in his letters that he used to hide to avoid being taken to the concerts. But the party was not always truly musical, and the diary notes on 20 November 1892: 'Got nearly mad over Master's guests talking in front row —I wish I wasn't so sensitive on that point.'

The diaries speak also of the Master's sermons in chapel: 'several of them are unorthodox but commonplace, always uttered in the Master's uniquely cherubic way'. One of them on Browning and the chief Balliol men who had died in the last six or seven years stands out. There is reference also to Jowett's lectures on Pre-Socratic philosophy to men just out of Mods. The lectures were held in the small lecture-room of the front quad which proved amply big for the few listeners. 'He specially sent and asked me as a favour to come. I suppose to set the example in asking questions.' It was scarcely a prospect to be enjoyed. The Master was old and tired, his strength was spent, and the glass of sherry and the biscuit that Perroud brought in half-way through the lecture failed to restore the spark of animation that made his private talk so vivid. Walker did his best about discussion, but things fell flat.

Walker was one of those privileged to stay with the Master in vacations. On three occasions he spent a week at Ashfield House, West Malvern, a Victorian red-brick house, where Jowett had established a former Balliol scout, retaining the right to go to it with his housekeeper and maid in Christmas and Easter vacations. Three or four Balliol men would be invited at a time. Here in Malvern, as the Master himself owned, conversation was freer than usually at Oxford. He was in the habit of sitting up late, and he was never seen till lunch time, when he appeared in his usual swallow-tail coat and bow tie. His hair was then snow-white, his complexion very pink, and his small cheeks fallen in.

The diaries tell 'the Master was in a lively mood and told stories that he evidently thought funny!' And later 'he is in wonderfully good health and spirits for a man nearly seventy-three. He hit hard all round in most animated political discussions, and told any number of stories usually with a sly knock at the ecclesiastical profession in them.'

Walker remembered how, on 31 December, Jowett, near midnight, rang the bell. There was a lengthy pause; the servants had presumably gone to bed and were getting up. At last a very sleepy maid appeared—Jowett in his high-pitched voice very brightly wished her a happy new year and ordered 'collations to celebrate the occasion suitably'—after a long interval a tray with sandwiches and a decanter were brought in. The wine was poured out in silence and somewhat shy wishes were uttered, but to the undergraduates then present this memory of the Master's friendliness remained vivid after sixty years.

A mental picture of Jowett in these days that never failed to amuse Walker was of the small man wearing a clerical coat ploughing up a Malvern Hill with snow on the ground, leaning on an alpenstock taller than himself. There is an affectionate touch in the entry: 'the dear old man seems to toddle about the hills in grand style'. On the 30th of December the Master left in the evening to attend Browning's funeral at Westminster, and Ernest Walker and Jimmy Palmer went off on one of their frequent sight-seeing expeditions, visiting Tewkesbury and Deerhurst —'a very curious and interesting early Saxon church— one of the very few still standing—which the Master was anxious for me to report on'.

Even after Walker had taken his degree the Master continued to ask for an essay every Thursday.

5 MAY 1892. Read essay about certainties and uncertainties of morals to the Master in evening, and got to a regular sort of talk on Christianity—truth of idea against truth of fact etc.

The Master summed up in a sentence which he added 'perhaps he would not say in public'—'that he did not know what Christianity would have become by now if it had not been for the Infidels'. And the keen personal interest the Master kept up in Walker's affairs was occasionally almost embarrassing.

Encaenia 1914: *in New College Cloisters with* RICHARD STRAUSS

Standing (from left to right): A. G. Heath, W. A. Pickard-Cambridge, B. C. Allchin, D. F. Tovey, H. P. Allen,
H. C. Colles, H. H. Turner, C. L. Stainer.
Seated: H. G. Fiedler, H. T. Gerrans, Edgar Speyer, Richard Strauss, Walter Parratt, C. B. Heberden,
Ernest Walker, J. Varley Roberts.
In front: G. F. Lawrence, Henry Ley.

Encaenia 1928 *with* MAURICE RAVEL

29 FEBRUARY 1892. Went to the Master. Some curious idea about my reading for a fellowship. . . . Music is the thing for me.

1 DECEMBER 1892. Took Essay on Law and Ethics to Master in evening, at which he practically ordered me to write for the English Essay on Erasmus next year. Confound it! Why should I waste my time like this?

But the end was coming. On 1 October 1893 the Master died:

Warrack one year, Nettleship the next, Jowett the next. Nothing like such a great man but he was wonderfully good to me all through these six years and one cannot realize what Balliol will be like without him.

Walker attended the funeral:

6 OCTOBER 1893. Up to Oxford for the Master's funeral—first part of service in Chapel and then a great impressive procession of 400 or so—all sorts of old Balliol men and other friends—to St. Sepulchre's cemetery where he was buried next to T. H. Green. Walked with Farmer and Pope directly behind the Fellows. . . . What a marvellous thing that Burial Service is!—still? But the whole experience was wonderful.

Jowett did not influence Walker greatly as a thinker or teacher, but his personality left on him, as on many others, a definite and deep impression.

The words of Andrew Bradley on the memorial tablet in Balliol Chapel describe Richard Lewis Nettleship. 'He loved great things and thought little of himself; desiring neither fame nor influence, he won the devotion of men and was a power in their lives; and seeking no disciples he taught to many the greatness of the world and of man's mind.'

There is no doubt that Ernest Walker was among those
to whom Nettleship was a lasting power in life. The influence was intangible and Walker could associate it with no
particular words, but there remained a vivid impression of
complete simplicity and single-mindedness, and at the same
time of a strongly passionate nature kept in firm control.
The diaries tell of lectures, discussions, and meetings for
music with Nettleship. Together they explored whole
volumes of Brahms's songs and other music—Nettleship
avoided selections—and their discoveries were often incor-
porated in Balliol programmes. The diaries of 1890 say:

Went through a good many Schumann Songs with Nettler—
really that man, although he has no particular voice, has one of the
rarest capacities for artistic conception and expression that I ever
knew. His singing is infinitely better than the majority of profes-
sionals, except that he has such a curious voice. If one forgets that,
it is really wonderful: and in conversation one finds that his entire
art-views are extraordinarily deep and pure, while his professorial
brother talks any amount about music, and knows hardly anything
about it from any point of view.

And soon after:

Played several Brahms Songs (*Romanzen* from *Tiecks Magelonen*
mainly) for Nettleship who seems to want to continue the habit:
and I certainly enjoyed it excessively—or perhaps 'enjoyed' is
hardly the word; if one was in a theological vein one would simply
thank God that a man had lived to write music which for its
glorious depth, poetry and earnestness, no artist, living or dead, has
ever surpassed.

And besides ploughing through complete volumes of composers at College, there was also music at old Mrs. Nettle-

ship's house, 7 Banbury Road, where Lewis Nettleship lived for the last years of his life and kept Jenny, his faithful dog-companion.

Much of Nettleship's self-forgetting outlook for Balliol was reflected in Walker's zeal for anything connected with the college. Prizes that Balliol men won were entered into his day-books, as well as athletic distinctions. He ran with a rattle along the tow-path cheering the College Eight, and after a bump-supper that Nettleship also attended, he banged about on an upright piano in the quad to support general revelry.

In tutorials and discussions the whole field of philosophy was covered by Nettleship, but Walker always regretted that he heard Nettleship lecture only on Aristotle, and never on Plato.

The letter which Nettleship wrote to Walker after the result of Greats was known reveals much of the writer's mind and of his care for his pupil's future. (It is perhaps worth remembering that Nettleship himself was unexpectedly placed in the second class in Greats.)

I have just been hearing about your work in the schools, and gather that you were very near a first. I know that this is poor consolation (if you *want* consolation) as far as the outside impression of the thing goes; but there is a certain satisfaction in knowing that one is practically in the same intellectual zone as the men whom one is accustomed to regard as 'first class men'.

Strachan-Davidson thinks that if you had been as good in scholarship as in other things, you would have been put in the first. However, I suppose and hope that you will soon be thinking of other things than classes. It has always been wonderful to me that with the spirit of music in you and about you, you could give so much of your mind to other things. I hope you don't feel that the music has suffered by it, for I should always feel that it is music that has the first claim on you. Of the many things that I cannot do, but can in a way imagine myself doing, it is that which always has the first place, and my favourite dream is that of getting to the heart of the world by song. It will be a great pleasure to me if you find yourself able to stay in Oxford for a time, though about this you ought of course to consult your own interests. It certainly seems as if there were a great field of activity here for a musician who has also an interest in men as well as in actual production.

For production alone Oxford can hardly be the most favourable place, I should think, either in music or anything else. But there is a sort of middle ground between the pure producer and the pure reproducer (though no doubt neither exists 'pure') which wants filling well. And in music as in other arts I am sure that any amount of good work can be done in the way of putting people on the way to understand and enjoy. It strikes me very much how the world is kept out of most of the best things by misunderstanding and not knowing how to begin. Most of what is called 'criticism' consists, it seems to me, in saying 'I A don't like you B' or 'you B have not done or said what I A think you ought to have done or said'. Of an honest attempt to get inside a man and tell other people what you found in him, there is almost nothing. Many of the people who have the power of appreciation have not the power of expression, and even if they have they seldom take the trouble of cultivating the two together.

After Walker took his degree the frequent meetings in Hall or at Nettleship's house continued. In 1891 both Walker's parents attended a Balliol Concert where his *De Profundis* was performed. Ernest's father especially enjoyed Farmer's appreciation of the music and Nettleship's co-operation among the tenors.

It was a great shock to Ernest to hear of Nettleship's

death through the columns of a newspaper in August 1892.
The diary says:

Apparently Nettleship and two guides, in ascending Mont Blanc
from Chamonix, were caught by a sudden storm near the Dôm
du Gouter, and the landmarks were so obliterated that they lost
their way, and after wandering about for a long time, they dug a
hole in the snow, and passed the night there, Nettleship 'singing
from time to time to prevent sleep'. In the morning the storm was
no better, but Nettleship preferred to try to descend rather than wait
for death; but after battling with the storm for an hour or so, the
cold and exhaustion overcame him and he sank and died 'after shak-
ing hands with the guides, and saying a few words in English not
understood by them'. And the guides somehow with great difficulty got down alive, and sent up others later to bring down the
body, which was buried at Chamonix August 29th.

In its way a truly grand ending, and worthy of one of the noblest
of men, who has done more to mould me than perhaps anyone else
in the world. Somehow I seemed to have got more than the majority of men at Balliol behind that wall of reserve which made him
seem to many so cold and unapproachable. And the memory of that
intimate intercourse of over three years seems now but a dream of
the great influence of a supremely earnest strong soul which indeed
'saw life steadily, and saw it whole'.

16 OCTOBER 1892. Sermon on Nettleship from the Master in
Chapel—characteristic production but the Master said himself, as
no doubt is true, that he never understood him.

One who was present remembers there was a sense of ten-
sion among the undergraduates in Chapel when Jowett had
the courage to confess 'I am afraid I did not always do
him justice because I did not altogether understand him'.
Walker went to see Mrs. Nettleship when he was back

in Oxford and continued regular visits twice a term, playing her favourite songs to her. She was devoted to him and called herself 'his affectionate grannie'. She entrusted to him the Shelley that her son had taken to Chamonix and the volumes of Brahms songs they had used together. Her companion wrote to Ernest Walker after her death (1898), 'Your music always made her so happy'.

About Charles Warrack there is little to say, but his influence in Balliol was a living force in Walker's time. Farmer spoke of him as the 'College Christ'.

He was not a Fellow and there is no memorial at Balliol to him, but the memory of this retiring scholar to whom philosophy was a real intellectual glow remained fresh in the minds of Ernest Walker and his generation.

5 DECEMBER 1890. Today Warrack's course of lectures— ostensibly on Logic, but really on the whole Aristotelian Logic, Metaphysics, and Psychology—came to an end. They have certainly been far the best lectures I have ever heard in Oxford— extremely clear exposition, and the justest and most interesting criticism; while through the whole there ran what I know now to be perhaps the chief point in a most fascinating character—a deep quasi-religious mysticism. From my three hours a week this term with him I have really come to admire the man wonderfully: a peculiarly 'spiritual' nature in the best sense (i.e. in the unorthodox sense) combined with acutest philosophical insight. For a real index to the man's character one should take, I think, his passion for Plotinus and Spinoza—and the concluding sentence of his lectures: 'To Aristotle all human thought is potentially divine: the true philosophic life is that in which man identifies himself with the world in the fullness of knowledge which is Love.'

15 SEPTEMBER 1891. Got a note from A. G. Little (an old Balliol man) at Chertsey saying that Warrack died there on Sunday last. Of course I knew that the man with that chest could probably not drag on very long, but still it gives one a shock to think that about the noblest man I ever knew has found out the secret of things for himself at last. Little asked me, as a friend of Warrack, to the funeral tomorrow afternoon, but I am afraid it will be impossible for me to manage it.

Warrack was little known outside Balliol, but it is obvious that Walker, like many of his contemporaries, had a profound admiration both for his teaching and for his personality.

3. Music 1887–1900

1. *A septet of Oxford musicians*

A SEPTET of strangely dissimilar personalities represented music in Oxford in 1887 when Ernest
Walker came to Balliol as an undergraduate.

Among them were manifold activities but there was less
public recognition than now, though music had been gaining a more respected place in the University than the
eighteenth century afforded, when artists were considered
mere craftsmen and servants to the nobility. In those days
(1792) an undergraduate tumult not infrequently interrupted a performance and it was deemed necessary to print
on notices that dogs should not be brought to the concerts.
An orange, aimed at a Holywell Music Room orchestra,
broke a Cremona violin as well as Malchair's career as the
leader. Even as late as about 1850, so the story goes, Dean
Gaisford burnt a chest of priceless viols stored in the Bod-
leian, supposing them to be dusty rubbish. The suspicion
that an undergraduate who had a piano in his room was
likely to come to a bad end lingered on, and Walker remembered how a delightful young aristocrat, who was trea-
surer of the Balliol Musical Society, accepted with genuine
alacrity the suggestion that envelopes containing fees
should be addressed 'Esq.'; 'Thank you for telling me; the
cricket team prefer it too.'

Jowett, though not musical himself had observed with
growing interest the ethical influence that John Farmer's

music-making had in Harrow where he had been Director of Music. Farmer, though unread in Plato, shared the Master's philosophical belief that music could be an influence for the bad as well as for the good. It was a feather in Farmer's cap that Jowett developed unwavering faith in him; for some time he resisted the call to Oxford, feeling tied to Harrow as long as Montagu Butler needed him there. When Butler became Master of Trinity, Cambridge, Farmer was free for the work that Balliol offered. No doubt the move to Oxford entailed much financial sacrifice for Farmer, but Jowett made conditions as attractive as possible: a house (21 Beaumont Street) was offered, and later on a study was thrown out at the back of it.

Farmer started his musical activities with characteristic enthusiasm. There was some floundering in those pioneering days: Farmer invited a brass band to play in the garden quad and got Jowett to be present. That experiment was not repeated. But the first secular Sunday concerts in England came to stay: Balliol started them in 1885, South Place in London followed in 1887. The Master acquired an organ for the Hall and since it was his gift, it was necessary to use it, but an upright piano was hoisted into the organ-loft to help out. Some Balliol undergraduates would take part (Dalhousie Young, George Simey, Harold Joachim, Francis Darbishire, and Ernest Walker) and the respected academic standing of most of these imperceptibly helped to establish a real appreciation of music rather than mere toleration both in the Master and in the college. The innovation of secular concerts on Sundays roused considerable

opposition in some quarters. The vicar of St. Mary Magda-
lene preached against practices 'which might be very well
in atheist Germany, but in Christian England and in my
parish. . . .' (Incidentally Balliol is extra-parochial.) Some
time later Farmer was much touched by a confession from
the vicar that he had been mistaken in attributing evil influence to the concerts. The music was good, on that score
Farmer was uncompromising and no doubt even the brass
band had been made to fall into line, but early Balliol programmes consisted mainly of snippets, with one movement, or at best two, from a great work adventured upon
now and again. Any hiatus in the programme could be
filled by calling upon Mary Farmer or her brother Gabriel
for a song to their father's accompaniment.

Among Farmer's other activities were 'Smoking Parlia-
ments' for about twenty undergraduates in one of the Senior
Common Rooms, but Ernest, who was never at any time
a smoker, did not go. His diaries, however, show frequent attendances at Hall-singing, held on Monday nights,
though he would go more in a sense of loyalty to Farmer
than because he had inclination for corporate jollity. Everything was lit up by Farmer's flamboyant personality, all of it
went with a swing and was healthy and inimitable. Frederick
Huth Jackson, who had sung Farmer's setting of 'Forty
Years On' with him at Harrow, now took a lead in smooth-
ing the way for 'The Balliol Rooks' and 'Verbum non
amplius Fisher' and other Balliol songs for which college
poets wrote the words.

Both for Chapel and for concerts Farmer made use of
Walker from the beginning and as terms went on he called

upon his help more and more. Walker also gave considerable time to reading the proof-sheets of Farmer's hymn
book. Perhaps it was over hymns that Farmer collided most
violently with his contemporaries. He never allowed anything sentimental in Chapel and he had no regard for asso-
ciation. In the book which he brought out he fitted fine
old tunes to words chosen by Jowett, Montagu Butler,
and others at his invitation.

When later the Bach Choir was started by Basil Har-
wood with more advanced musical claims, Farmer still went
on gallantly with Hall-singing, undaunted by smaller attendances. A paralytic stroke laid him by eighteen months
before his death, July 1901. At the beginning of Farmer's
illness Walker was asked by the college to act as deputy
organist and given to understand that this would mean his
ultimate succession to the post of organist. Hall-singing
had fulfilled its end by then and anyhow was not Walker's
métier.

How much Farmer relied upon Walker's help and how
completely he believed in him becomes clear in letters. In
writing to Mrs. Walker in 1891 to thank her for the present
of a red malacca cane, which became his constant companion, he says:

We are greatly indebted to your son Ernest. During his four
years at Balliol he has composed so much really beautiful music for
us; has helped us so modestly, patiently and powerfully in the cause
of good music. The Master and the whole College are grateful to
him for what he has done. I am deeply indebted to him. When I
was so ill he did me the kindest service. My wife and family will
always remember it.

And again after an illness in 1895 he wrote to Walker himself:

I can't thank you enough for your kindness with respect to the Society of Arts business. It is a good work done. The remembrance of some events of the exam. come back to me like a dream. When I was feeling ill and depressed the thought crossed my mind of my not being able to see the medal people again and my soul felt blowy. I am now in better spirits. I can't write what I want to say. I know how patiently you always read between the lines of my clumsy ways.

I must keep the High School Concert and Exam. notices for next month. Better for them to appear during term time.

I am so grateful to have you to depend on for keeping the kettle boiling of this great advantage for doing good, helping those to whom help will be a blessing. The girl who could sing 'He was despised' like we heard it will be of more use to the world than all the negative critical Josephs put together.

Go on composing. If you have the courage to go on fearlessly in spite of your dread of failure you will before ten years are over do something that England will be proud of.

This stimulating outlook, and generous appreciation meant a great deal to Walker, but Farmer took no interest in degree work and possessed no technical mastery that he could pass on to others. So for the final B.Mus. examination Ernest went for two terms for coaching to Dr. Frederick Iliffe, Organist of St. John's, at his private house. Here in a room, almost entirely taken up by a pipe organ and a grand piano, they would sit at two tiny square tables spread with music paper, Dr. Iliffe pencilling suggestions into the score that Walker had brought with him. It was honest, good grind, and well worth doing. Iliffe's choir at St. John's was of no account, and the ramshackle organ there allowed no display; but as a teacher he was very thorough and took limitless trouble over his many pupils. After the examination he wrote congratulations to Walker disclaiming any credit to himself in the success: 'You did it all yourself.'

Iliffe was quiet, shy, without any pretensions to creative gift, but possessing supreme skill in mechanical craftsmanship: the industrious under-dog, modest and content to be it.

The leading musician of Oxford in 1887 was Dr. Charles Lloyd of Christ Church. He was reputed the best improvisor in England and possessed great skill as an organist; his general musicianship was competent rather than outstanding. He conducted the little local orchestra led by Mary Venables, but owing to his highly strung temperament and quick nervous movements it remained a humdrum affair. Arthur Benson once said of Lloyd, who afterwards went to Eton, 'of course we all of us have to struggle with the beast within us, but I think Lloyd has to struggle with the bird within him'. On one occasion the little orchestra was fitted into Balliol Hall for a concert and Walker was invited to contribute Schumann's *Papillons* to lengthen their programme. Dates for concerts given in the Sheldonian had to be chosen with great care in days before artificial lighting; one dark November afternoon Beethoven's Seventh Symphony was finished to a great extent by heart, not a very successful effort, but still reflecting some credit on the players who kept going when Dr. Lloyd's baton was scarcely visible.

Walker went to Dr. Lloyd for organ lessons as some skill was needed for Balliol Chapel services. Lloyd's teaching was desultory and his choice of pieces was far too hard for beginners and Walker never developed a secure technique on organ pedals. However, by dint of improvising voluntaries he held his own: in this way a miskick might be converted into an unusual harmony whilst the manuals obediently followed suggestions that came unpremeditatedly from the pedals.

At New College James Taylor was the organist. He was a pupil of Sterndale Bennett and his pianism was remarkable: clear-cut, clean, of the restrained type, that showed to advantage in Mendelssohn's G minor Concerto. He was the leading piano-teacher of the Oxford of his day; essentially shy and never successful as a conductor of the orchestra or Choral Society and content with adequate achievement for the New College choir. His gentle, dignified manner compelled cordial esteem from all sides; his gifted family too were well known. His daughters Leila and May, who played the violin and the 'cello, performed at Balliol Sunday concerts with Walker. One son, Colin, became the Head of the Conservatoire in Cape Town, another, Leonard, won renown as an R.A. and his memorable painting 'The Rehearsal' was bought for the Tate Gallery by the Chantrey Bequest.

At Magdalen John Varley Roberts trained the choir; a bluff good-natured Yorkshire man who merited his wide reputation for choosing his singers and getting the best out of them. In his broad north-country accent he would boast with justifiable pride that his chief bass John Lomas (capable of a gorgeous 'cello-like sound on the low C) had remained loyal to himself and Magdalen in spite of manifold efforts to bribe him away. Roberts's organ playing was poor, devoid of technique and second-rate in taste; in solemn marches a favourite effect of his was a queer deep rumble produced by swaying up and down the keys with his left fore-arm on a sixteen-foot Bourdon. Little wonder, in that acoustically perfect chapel, that a Friday, with its unaccompanied singing, was the day musicians chose to hear the choir; it was generally considered the finest in England, indeed famous throughout the world. Roberts dedicated the best part of his life to attain for Magdalen this high distinction, but only at the end of his days did the Senior Common Room pay him the tribute of admitting him to membership, an indication of the attitude towards music in those days.

Besides these professional musicians there were dons who as amateurs took a prominent part in the music of the University. At the Oxford University Musical Club Henry Hadow was supported by Harold Joachim, Paul Benecke, Franklin Harvey, and Ernest Walker; Farmer's activities were restricted to Balliol and he rarely made use of his honorary membership. The Club, with its headquarters at 115 High Street, possessed a library and organized Tuesday evening concerts. The President, virtually a dictator for concert arranging, was appointed for a whole year, and Walker was elected in 1892 and 1897. The Public Classical Concerts were founded as an off-shoot of the Club, and Hadow's gifts as an organizer were freely given to this venture. Most of the leaders of the Oxford University Musical Club primarily represented academic subjects, and helped to create an understanding for music in the University; but none mingled their knowledge more completely with music than Hadow. His lectures in the Sheldonian given 'for the Heather Professor of Music' in his rapid, eager delivery, bubbled over with humour and shone with the fire of a proselytizer. Comparatively elementary musical facts were illuminated with unknown brilliance and the full panoply of philosophical knowledge and wide reading in many languages was drawn upon for picturesque detail. Walker frequently provided illustrations at the piano for these lectures, which attracted undergraduates and a large general public. The publication of Hadow's *Studies in Modern Music* marked an era, gaining an acknowledged place for music in general culture, and establishing claims for the amateur at his best, a service to music which he further substantiated as editor and writer and extended during his later distinguished career as administrator in education. Hadow's songs found favour in Oxford homes; aware of his own limitations as a composer he would ward off praise and assert in his emphatic way that Ernest Walker's music would stand the test of time.

Dr. John Henry Mee, Fellow of Merton, Tutor in Ancient History, and Precentor of Chichester, was a considerable figure in the world of Oxford music at that time. From Kettel Hall, and later from the big house he built in

Jowett Walk (nicknamed 'Palazzo Mee' or 'The Meum', now the School of Geography) he extended social support to undergraduate chamber music. Almost as a protest to the Oxford University Musical Club he founded the Musical Union that met in the big room behind Taphouse's shop, and somewhat indiscriminatingly gave opportunities to undergraduate enterprise. There was a wish to secure talent for the Union and Dr. Mee, having heard about Ernest Walker, sent Mr. Arthur Foxton-Ferguson to Anerley to bespeak him as a member of the Union before he had started residence at Balliol. But once in Oxford, Walker joined the Oxford University Musical Club and neither he, nor Hadow, was ever a 'Mee's man', though their compositions were given a hearing at the Union. Walker could remember the days when the University regulations, that Donald Tovey described in his essays on 'the training of the Musical Imagination', still held good, and the 'exercise' for the doctor of music had to be performed in public. In many cases some very perfunctory performances must have been put on, the poor composer no doubt hoping no one would hear them; Stainer abolished the tradition as one of his first acts when he became Professor of Music. But when Johnnie Mee took his degree he engaged a professional orchestra and first-class soloists and the Leeds Choir, and conducted his B flat *Missa Solemnis* before a crowded Sheldonian. Professor Ouseley, sitting near the first violin, followed with a full score, thus testifying for the University that the work performed was identical with the exercise sent in for the degree. This brilliant setting was curiously out of proportion to the dull, wooden work so magnificently decked out.

Thus Walker was brought into contact with many different musical personalities in his early days. Each and all had some influence on him, but the greatest force in determining his career was without doubt that of Farmer.

II. *Musical experiences*

There are many entries about music in the diaries, which give early evidence both of Walker's single-minded enthusiasm and of his critical insight. Unconsciously he was training himself as a writer on music. Most of these refer to activities and experiences in Oxford.

3 MAY 1892. Took Nettleship and F. M. to Club in evening— Schumann's on the whole very inferior F major Quartet, Beethoven's Violin Sonata in E flat (op. 12, no. 3), not one of his most inspired, and Brahms's new Clarinet Quintet in B minor (Egerton, and Gibson leading). Farmer had lent me the score but still of course one would like another hearing; but on a first it seems one of Brahms's finest things, I think. A marvellous slow movement, of a decidedly Hungarian colour.

13 SEPTEMBER 1892. Played over the fifth and sixth volumes of Simrock's edition of selected Brahms songs—which I got at Novello's yesterday. A good many of the finest, which I have known from going over them with Miss Farmer or Nettleship, are still not in— such as 'Herbstgefühl', 'O kühler Wald', 'Mit vierzig Jahren' etc., etc.; besides all those published by others than Simrock: but I came across one superb one, that I did not know before—'Meerfahrt' a most weirdly passionate setting of Heine's extraordinarily imaginative 'Mein Liebchen wir saßen beisammen'—one of the greatest of these marvellous gems of vague flawless beauty—informulate 'Sehnsucht'—which are all about the *Buch der Lieder*.

4 OCTOBER 1892. More music with Briggs and Bucknall—every-

thing went really very nicely, though Bucknall, with all his artistic feeling, has not very much technique—Brahms C major Trio twice over, and the C minor Trio twice over too. Certainly the latter improves on acquaintance enormously; still there is nothing in it as deep as the Andante of the C major, though it is a singularly charming (and in the first movement very massive) and decidedly less severe work.

31 OCTOBER 1892. An hour's Brahms with Miss Farmer in Hall in afternoon—many old favourites, and also several that I had not been over with her or anyone else before. No doubt some are inclined to be heavy—but one doesn't expect the man to be always perfect, and I came across some superb ones I did not know—a weirdly beautiful setting of a weird Eichendorff poem 'Anklänge' (from op. 7) and a very elaborate and imaginative 'Abenddämmerung'.

4 NOVEMBER 1892. Reading and practising as usual. An hour's Schumann and Brahms with Miss Farmer in Hall in afternoon— how strange it is, taking the 'Schwanengesang', that one or two (like the 'Ständchen' and 'Fischermädchen') have become so hackneyed, while others *at least* equally fine, like 'Ihr Bild', 'In der Ferne', 'Die Stadt' and—to my mind, perhaps, the greatest song in all music— 'Am Meer', are heard in public rarely, if ever: while as for things of Brahms like some of those we did today, e.g. 'Der Kuss', 'An eine Äolsharfe', 'Die alte Liebe', 'Während des Regens', 'O komme, holde Sommernacht'—when does one hear them?

30 NOVEMBER 1892. Grand Concert—Corn Exchange in evening—*very* miscellaneous music, as usual at Grand Concerts. Jean Gerardy—a real mature artist, with lovely tone and style—played some poor things: a Mademoiselle Torac 'the eminent Belgian violinist' played the Finale from Grieg's F major (the stock thing for such occasions) and other pieces with spirit and intelligence, but nothing at all remarkable. Miss Evangeline Florence sang rubbish with a voice of beautiful quality and marvellous compass, from the

low 'A' to a perfectly effortless and sweet and full high 'G', while her high A's and C's were like a flute for purity and roundness. The other singers, Miss Marie Brema and Messrs. Wade and Ley—and Mr. Waddington Cook—'call for no serious comment'. As a matter of fact they were hopelessly bad, and I am afraid the manners of Miss Farmer who was just in front of us, and Jimmy and I who happened to be together, cannot have pleased the very ardent admirers of the third-rate performers, and general fourth-rate music. I came away after the first half.

But Walker was now getting outside Oxford and the diary tells of visits to London. One was to hear Sarah Bernhardt:

9 JULY 1892. To London by myself this afternoon to English Opera House, Shaftesbury Avenue. Dumas, *La Dame aux Camélias*. The company on the whole was only fair, M. Henry's 'Armand' being the best; but no words can describe the magic of the Marguerite Gautier of Sarah Bernhardt herself—the marvellous loveliness of her voice—the extraordinary charm of every play of her features and every movement of her body—the almost maddening seductiveness of the whole. And yet there is nothing in the slightest degree exaggerated or strained—it is simply overpowering reality. The way in which she can say a word or two—like 'Oh l'amour! l'amour!' at the end of the first act—simply makes one's head swim. And the woman who can look like that must be nearly fifty.

Other visits were to the operas conducted by Gustav Mahler, and in particular to Wagner productions.

13 JULY 1892. Up to London at Covent Garden again in evening—*Die Götterdämmerung*. No doubt there are supreme things in the score, such as the 'Trauermarsch', and wonderful moments scattered all about; and the ingenuity and imagination of the work-

manship, and the beauty and dramatic force of the 'motives' is marvellous—but as a whole the work left me with a decided feeling of oppression. It did not strike me as altogether equal to the *Walküre* or *Siegfried*, still less *Tristan*—the greatest of all—but still I remember how many works, such as the great things of Brahms—often seem dull at first, and only unfold their wonder and their worth on intimate knowledge.

The 'Norns' Scene was entirely omitted but at any rate it is not necessary in the drama and without it the thing lasted five hours. The stage arrangements were again *miserable*—certainly one would not have understood the end a bit without knowing the libretto beforehand: the pyre was burning all right, but Brunhilde and her horse quietly went off at the wings, and the Rhine and the Rhine daughters were altogether non-existent.

20 JULY 1892. Last of my seven German operas at Covent Garden this evening—*Fidelio*. Of course it is impossible to compare it in any way with the Wagner things: for it is an opera, and the others are 'music-dramas', and there is all the difference in the world. Again it would be an anachronism to expect in an opera of 1805 that subservience of everything to dramatic truth which one finds in Wagner and which—as in parts of *Tristan* in its marvellous welding together of words and music—make one forget that apart from the emotions expressed by the words, the music would probably be very uninteresting. But still there is a very considerable amount indeed of dramatic force in *Fidelio*—all over the place—certainly much more than in Mozart—and with music of absolute beauty the score is crowded—the Prisoners' chorus in the first act being perhaps the most marvellous. But still I must say that I don't think Beethoven's genius is most seen on the stage; the *Leonora No. 3*—perhaps the most absolutely perfect thing in all music—is worth all the opera put together. For the expression of supremely exultant passion I defy anything in the world to equal the close; and good God! it looks so simple, and yet it makes one bury one's face in one's hands

and tremble.... The orchestra was very good, though the drums made an appalling row at times; and the performance of *Leonora No. 3* was extremely unconventional, and in its way, very fine; though I did not at all agree with Mahler's occasional 'tempo rubato'. That sort of thing does not do in Beethoven.

Other occupations were also crowding in on Walker. In 1892 when he was twenty-two, he wrote an article on Brahms's songs, which was accepted for the *Musical Times* —the beginning of his career as a writer on music—and the diary of 31 October 1892 records a visit with Farmer to the Oxford High School 'to accompany my part-songs in his class of girls there, who really read them very nicely'. This led to examination-work at girls' schools, for Farmer's Harrow School of Music, for the Girls' Public Day Schools Trust, and for the Society of Arts.

Moreover Reginald Carter the editor of the *Oxford Magazine* secured him for reporting on music and Walker kept to this work till 1924, the guinea a term originally offered dropping out from 1914. His articles make good reading. They give a telling account of Oxford music and are made vivid with amusing thumb-nail sketches. His writing was very pointed but there is record too of great enthusiasm; as Donald Tovey put it, 'there is little of beauty or worth that eludes Ernest'. The *Manchester Guardian* and *The Times* sounded Walker for reporting work but his love of Oxford was all-powerful. The hectic, up-to-time routine of newspaper staff-work in a big town could scarcely present temptations to one so acutely sensitive to beauty in nature, and so able to mirror her moods in song.

Farmer, who was untiring in his zeal to put Walker's gifts

to good use, secured him for his friend, Joseph Williams's new venture the *Musical Gazette*. It was an idealistic publication, no advertisements were admitted and Walker had a free hand as its editor with one strange exception; Joseph Williams tolerated no adverse criticism of Gounod's *Redemption* on the ground that this work was Novello's best seller, and his chivalry forbade possible injury to a friendly publishing firm through the columns of one of his own publications. Farmer had hoped to secure a large public for the *Musical Gazette* by recommending girls' schools to send up notices of their doings, but the sale, never very large, soon dwindled. The haphazard dates of publication that Mr. Williams chose puzzled even its loyal readers and after ten numbers the *Gazette* died. During its life-time it upheld a fine standard. It had the distinction of sponsoring what were probably Tovey's first printed works, an analysis of Brahms's C minor pianoforte quartet, and 'Performance and Personality' a critical essay on Joachim and Dohnanyi. Hadow gave a telling sketch of 'Music in a Hungarian Coffee House' and Florence May 'Reminiscences of Brahms as a teacher'. Walker wrote the greater part of most numbers himself, filling in gaps with short articles that show the outlook that he held all his life. His longest contribution was the obituary essay on Farmer; on the whole the Press was grossly unfair to Farmer, and Mrs. Burnet (Mary Farmer) wrote gratefully to Walker for the only just estimates, his portraits of Farmer in the *Musical Herald* and *Musical Gazette*.

The reputation as an accompanist that Walker had gained at the Balliol Concerts led to many engagements in

London and the provinces, which brought acquaintance—
and often close friendship—with many artists. The songs
which Walker composed during these years were often sung
by Marie Fillunger, Gervase Elwes, and Plunket Greene.
The last named had a peculiar affection for them; he wrote
once: 'I take off my hat to Spring Twilight.' His steady
phrasing of 'Sweet Obscurity' remained a treasured memory
for Walker. Only in 'Snowdrops'—to which the composer
had added metronome markings—did the pace Plunket
Greene inflicted cause regrets. However, his rendering of
'Hey Nonny No' was terrifying with its almost intoxicating
passion, and 'Corinna's Going a-Maying', always at break-
neck speed, seemed to find its place in almost all his
programmes. He made it blaze with life. Gervase Elwes
sang 'The Wind on the Wold' and 'Come into the Garden, Maud' and captured the delicate urge of 'Bluebells
from the Clearings', which has often suffered from being
sentimentalized. This last song was given the prize offered
by Charles Phillips in 1909: several hundred composers
had entered for it, including Gustav Holst.

Perhaps the most remarkable of these musical friendships was with Casals, the famous 'cellist. Walker met him
first in July 1898 at a private party in Kensington and
played his accompaniments. Shortly afterwards Casals (by
introduction of the Queen of Spain) was invited to play at
Osborne and he asked Ernest Walker to come with him. In
those days Casals could not speak a word of English, and
Walker's French was pressed into service. The artists went
from Southampton to Cowes and were put up in a small
hotel on the east side of the Medina river, the ferry to the

more fashionable west side not being in action in the evening hours. Quite a good little dinner with cheerful talk was just finished when the royal carriage called for the drive to Osborne. Here they were received by footmen who conducted them through long passages to a fairly large room with full-length paintings of the Prince Consort in Highland shooting kit with dead prey all round him. The footmen vanished after saying that Lord Edward Pelham-Clinton would summon the artists. Casals and Ernest Walker sat down and waited for about half an hour, the sense of expectation too strong upon them for a chat. At last footsteps: Lord Edward Pelham-Clinton appeared in court dress: then more and more passages, more and more pictures of the Prince Consort, Casals silently carrying his 'cello, Walker following with the music-case. Then a halt before the last of a series of gilt-handled doors. Lord Edward Pelham-Clinton opened the door, and the three walked straight into the presence of Queen Victoria who was sitting at a large table by herself, with Princess Beatrice and the Duke of Connaught on her right. There were about thirty people in the room, all in uniform or court dress. The queen was in full evening dress, the low cut showing her very white skin; she looked dignified and impressive to a degree that no photograph could convey. Ernest Walker was genuinely impressed with her personality. The Queen finished her talk with an admiral and then picked up her large hand-written programme as a sign that the music should start. Walker took his seat at the Chickering Grand from Boston, U.S.A., and noticed, whilst Casals was tuning, that the pedal squeaked. There was whispering in the audience, but the Queen signalled for attention and in complete silence Fauré's *Elegy* was played. The music went on for about half an hour (Saint-Saens's *Allegro* in B minor, an old Italian sonata), with no applause, but in the intervals between the pieces the Queen spoke German to Princess Beatrice. When the programme was finished Casals was beckoned forward, and the Queen in French thanked him and inquired what was the small red order that he wore on his coat. Then Casals stepped back, and Walker was beckoned forward, and the Queen said, 'You accompany very beautifully' and added a few relevant remarks about the music. When it was evident that the concert was over, two six-foot Indians came and grasped the Queen's arms, and helped her slowly, inch by inch, to get up from her chair, and leaning on her Indians she left the room. Then Lord Edward Pelham-Clinton stepped forward and handed a case of gold sleeve-links to Casals, and to Walker a silver cigarette case with 'from V.R.I.' and a crown inlaid in colour. The Duke of Connaught said some words in what purported to be Spanish, but Casals confessed later he did not understand them.

Once more the artists were conducted by footmen down passages till they reached a room with supper for two. Casals wanted to say good-bye to Lord Edward Pelham-Clinton, but the footman could not find him. On his search he took Casals and Walker into a billiard-room where a game was going on, but even that failed to produce him, so without a farewell the artists were taken to the carriage and driven to the hotel. The next morning, after a very early breakfast, Mr. Philip Yorke appeared with the royal birthday book which both artists signed at the queen's request. Filled with the glow of success Casals went to telegraph an account of his visit to his relatives in Spain, and Walker needed all his most urgent French to cope with the difficulties of extracting him from the post office in time to catch the steamer.

About fifty years later Casals wrote on 28 January 1947.

Cher Dr. Walker,

Votre lettre ne pouvait pas me faire plus de plaisir. Les inoubliables temps de ma jeunesse et partant des commencements de ma carrière s'attachent à votre nom et à votre personne—Il va sans dire qu'en écrivant ma lettre à l'Éditeur du Times vous étiez présent.

Quel plaisir qu'à mon âge, nous pouvions encore correspondre et caresser de si vieux et chers souvenirs—Je ne peux pas m'empêcher d'établir un autre trait d'union entre vous et moi, celui de *notre* amitié et dévotion pour cet être extraordinaire qu'était Sir D. F. Tovey, notre cher Donald. Souvent j'ai dans mes mains ces précieux petits volumes—'A Musician Talks'—que vous avez préfacés—Je suis toujours attiré par ce parfait portrait de Donald le musicien et les diverses caractéristiques de l'homme—c'est vous dire que je me plais à lire cette Préface qui me réunit toujours avec la même émotion avec vous et avec lui.

Acceptez, cher Dr. Walker, les meilleurs sentiments et vœux de votre tout devoué

Pau Casals.

III. *The University: Teacher and examiner*

Ernest Walker's activities and interests during these years were by no means confined to Balliol. In Oxford he was a well-known figure and had a strong guiding influence in the development of music. He was greatly in demand as a pianist and accompanist at the Public Subscription Concerts, the Oxford University Musical Club, and the Ladies' Musical Society. He was an influential member of the Committees of the Subscription Concerts, the Bach Choir, and the Musical Club, and to the affairs of the last he devoted much time and attention. He was its President on more than one occasion and for twenty years acted as Librarian. He went daily to read the Library entries and did all the labelling and the issuing of notices when books were not returned punctually. There was an occasion when a member had taken a volume out of another member's room without entering his name in the Library register; all that was known of the man who had purloined the book was that he wore a college tie. Walker wrote personal notes to the fifteen men of that college who were members of the Musical Club explaining the situation. Fourteen wrote back indignantly protesting letters and the book was at once returned anonymously. There were storms of applause when Walker reported the incident in a speech to the general meeting.

In 1918 he catalogued the Nash Library single-handed, at a time when it was temporarily stored in Taphouse's upper room, the Army Medical Service having taken over the Holywell Music Room. He dealt with every book and all the sheet music.

At the head of every page in the Club Register he wrote in bold letters, 'The attention of borrowers is called to the rules to be obeyed by them'. There are many entries of music taken out by H. P. Allen and put back by Ernest Walker; music was lost and found in unexpected places; in college rooms, or organ-lofts, and once in the middle of the road near Wallingford.

During Walker's life-time a great change came over the position of music in the University and the official attitude towards it. When Walker came up and for many years afterwards, residence was not required for the B.Mus. degree. The candidate came to Oxford to do some papers in music and an 'additional subject', which was usually a modern language. It was not till 1927 that residence was demanded, and later still that a B.Mus. was required to be a B.A. as well, though the two examinations could be dove-tailed. Similarly for a long time the tuition and examinations in music were under the control of a Board of Studies, and it was not till 1945 that the Faculty of Music was established with an independent position alongside the other Faculties.

From the first Walker was eager to improve the position of music, the regulations for the examinations, and the organization of teaching. For long there was opposition not only from outside, but from fellow musicians. But Walker received strong support when in 1901 H. P. Allen was appointed Organist of New College. The two men were of very different temperaments, but they had the same aims as regards the status of music in the University. Walker's reviews always reflect his warm appreciation of Allen's organ recitals, their interesting choice of works, and speak of his growing reputation as a choral and orchestral conductor.

Walker's fine musicianship and professional standards and Allen's dominating personality made a strong combination which could secure for the study of music a notable place in the University. Between them great things were achieved. How much the smooth working of this combination was due to Ernest Walker's fortitude is best left unestimated. In 1918 Allen was appointed Heather Professor of Music at Oxford and nominated Walker as Choragus for the next four years; till then it had been a life appointment but Allen expressed a wish that it should be held by different Oxford musicians for a few years at a time.

Allen had a great admiration for Walker and often spoke to other musicians in terms which showed that he was fully aware of his great gifts of musicianship and character; he noticeably deferred to Walker's opinion in meetings of the Board of Studies and of the Faculty of Music. But Allen was brusque and had a strain of the bully in him strangely mingled with a deep but sometimes autocratic kindness; his 'unmerciful ragging' was always at its worst with Oxford artists more sensitive and distinguished than himself. During the long years of co-operation there were no doubt many unblemished memories, yet in his last mellower years Allen often regretted what he realized to have been something like cruelty to his colleagues, and when, in 1942, the Cobbett Gold Medal of the Worshipful Company of Musicians was conferred on Walker, Sir Hugh was frankly anxious to make the presentation particularly festive, and no doubt his influence had counted in making the award. He stressed that on this occasion the medal had been won three times over; it could be awarded for the composition of chamber music, or the performance of it, or the arranging of concerts. And here, in Ernest Walker's case, there were ample qualifications under each heading. The presentation of the medal by the Grand Master, Sir Stanley Marchant, took place at a New College tea-party. It was simple, friendly, and much enjoyed. In telling about it Ernest Walker was tranquil and serene, Sir Hugh blusteringly enthusiastic. To both men it had been a pleasurable event.

Up to the end of the summer term of 1914 concerts prospered as usual and Walker was always their heart and soul. And then in August came the sudden change. Walker went out of his way to find war work he could undertake usefully. At one time he gave five to six hours a day to National Registration; the entire female population of Oxford passed through his hands. Mecelias, Didos, and Junos were common in the St. Barnabas district, but Terpsichore Dorcas Chinchan Ubinger was the prize find among names!

There was an odd episode in July 1918: Walker was summoned to attend for military medical inspection, was given two shillings and told to await further orders. Nothing more happened; however, he enjoyed the joke that having been accepted and having never been dismissed, he remained a member of the army even in old age.

His real contribution to the war effort was to uphold music and maintain a sane and balanced outlook. From 1914–18 Walker kept the Balliol Concerts in being with the help of musical cadets and local talent. Drawing mainly on his own resources he provided music on Sunday evenings, soldiers forming the bulk of his audiences. At many concerts German music was banned; but Walker often played his own piano version of the wonderful epilogue of Richard

Strauss's *Don Quixote*, both at Balliol and at girls' schools, and he included a Reger Memorial at one concert making a short speech on the death of the great composer in Germany and playing some of his music. The soldiers applauded warmly. This Balliol Concert may perhaps have been the only token of respect paid to Reger's musicianship in England in 1916.

As soon as Walker had gained his doctorate (Nov. 1898) Stainer put down his name as one of the teachers for the University, but for years this was purely formal. Later he was, of course, one of the regular tutors. At one time he had a good many piano pupils but his heart was more in his harmony teaching. There he tried to carry out Stanford's ideal of doing strict exercises and free composition side by side, allowing an unusual degree of freedom in the free, but rigorously avoiding the mixing of styles. He was glad to accept Parratt's decision that he was to handle the subject of harmony liberally, for he had little use for prolonged drill in rigid counterpoint.

The teaching of harmony slowly increased and generations of young musicians in their impressionable years came under Walker's unobtrusive influence. It was not so much that they shared his enthusiasm but that they came to adopt his approach to music. He had so high a sense of artistic integrity and professional standard because he was more of an artist than a craftsman and he certainly made known to many what a sensitive musician can do with music. Some pupils remembered 'the alert mind and nimble wit' and his self-forgetting interest in their problems. Others recalled how he would dash to any other room in the house and would return almost at once with a book that contained some passage illuminating the discussion. He tried hard to move the burdened plodder away from conscientious struggles, into habits of grasping essentials and living on the enjoyment of a personal outlook to each work of art. He himself was rapid in discovering the most beautiful and telling pages in a work, and he would be frankly surprised to find a pupil ploughing stolidly ahead from page one, before taking the bearings of the composition or book. He taught many to make intelligent use of an index, to let the habit of glancing at the general character of a composition or book precede the reading of it. He always caused pupils to take note of the words before plunging into the music of a song; he would warn against wasting too much time on completeness especially in editions of minor men ('for most of us life is too short for them'), and would deprecate the uncritical catalogue outlook that merely accumulates facts. His idea was to make his pupils self-reliant in discovering what sounded well.

The character and influence of his teaching have been described by several of his pupils. Dr. Thomas Armstrong in the *Musical Times* for March 1949 wrote:

Walker's influence as a teacher was largely dependent upon his work as an artist. He had been brought up in a time of strict principles, and was by nature a sceptic, who submitted all the accepted rules to a highly critical examination. His experience as a practical musician had given him immense respect for the classical tradition, as a living art, with its own contemporary masters and obligations. Modern practices with him had to be tested with respect to classical tradition, classical principles had to be interpreted in the light of modern achievements. Any 'rule' had to show its credentials before gaining admittance. Walker was admittedly a better teacher for the gifted man than for the dull one.

Walker never bluffed, and was deeply musical, and this made him specially effective with the sensitive, sceptical, or rebellious type of young man. There were not a few of this kind who found, like Philip Heseltine, a sympathetic understanding in Walker which they did not find elsewhere. And it was to Walker that many of them returned again and again in after years to renew old enthusiasms and to seek fresh guidance.

A more intimate sketch is given in a letter from Professor W. K. Stanton:

I got to know Ernest Walker in my first fortnight in Oxford. He had heard of me through a mutual friend, and took early opportunity of asking me to his house. I confess that, as a raw stripling, I was not a little alarmed at the prospect of 'thé à deux'—but he soon dispelled my fears by his welcome and friendly greeting. At that time, Oxford did not recognize those poor creatures who wished to read music seriously; consequently the University arranged no instruction for musical degrees: but, later on, provision was made, and I became Walker's pupil.

To be taught by him was a privilege. I remember so well his insistence on standards: his impeccable taste: his anger at anything shoddy: his sense of fun. There was always a kindly toleration for our inexperience: a gentleness in his criticism of our excursions (probably very hazardous) into what was then up-to-date harmonic fashion, but which is now long obsolete.

Above all I remember his unfailing kindness to young undergraduates like myself: and his eager discussion of interesting points about the music we had heard at concerts. I met him one day, the day after a recital by Harold Bauer, and asked him what he had thought of the performance. He was obviously very much impressed by Bauer's sensitive pedalling—and said, 'My dear Stanton, the tone he gets with his feet'! His excitement was expressed both visibly and audibly.

But Walker's interest did not end when the young undergraduate proceeded to a degree and departed from Oxford. On the contrary, it never flagged, and in my case the friendship formed in 1909 continued till his death. He was a fine teacher, one of the most sensitive musicians I have known, and a real friend.

Before examinations Walker would invite pupils to a race in copying music; he himself could cover ground very quickly and he emphasized the advantage of speed for examinations. He remembered how he did not manage to get his own answers completely copied in his B.Mus. examination before Parry, who was examining, put out a large hand and confiscated the unfinished paper.

With pupils who were not essentially musical Walker was very patient and kind, but he might find it difficult to see what it was that befogged them; he was almost too generous in considering some of their blunders a mere 'slip of the pen'.

A list of Walker's pupils would be a very long one, including in fact all who read for musical degrees in the years when he was teaching. Perhaps the most famous was William Walton, but in his undergraduate days at Christ Church he was rather unapproachable, almost resenting help and neither Allen nor Walker nor anyone else guessed to what lengths he would go. A few other names may be chosen almost at random: Adrian Boult, Thomas Armstrong, Reginald Jacques, William Harris, H. G. Ley, William McKie, Frank Howes, Victor Hely-Hutchinson, Trevor Harvey, Sydney Watson, Sidney Newman.

Two of his private pupils were Graham Peel and Ernest Frankel. With Peel an intimate friendship was formed; he was a shy, attractive undergraduate at University College, very gentle, tall and fair, with lots of polish of manner.

All Peel's earlier songs were shown to Walker and the half pedalling in 'Bredon Hill' was his suggestion. Peel's songs and settings, particularly his 'Twa Sisters of Binnorie' were often sung at Balliol by Campbell McInnes, and Walker enjoyed the piano accompaniment that allowed his soft harp effect, a quick arpeggio ending in clenching the fist. He also remembered many happy visits to the home that McInnes and Peel shared.

Walker had a warm regard for Ernest Frankel, who besides reading for Modern Greats found time for serious music and became president of the Oxford University Musical Club. After leaving Trinity College he came from London to 28 St. Margaret's Road about once a fortnight for composition lessons and discussions. These talks remained confined to music but none the less a great friendship was formed; Frankel developed a considerable technique in miniature work, and, at Walker's suggestion, the Oxford University Press published one of his settings of Elizabethan lyrics—delicate, sensitive musically and harmonically, under the influence of Delius. His death (when killed at the head of his men in Africa) was a very great blow to Walker. Mrs. Frankel wrote of her son: 'He was very grateful to you and always looked so happy when he spoke of you.'

Besides his teaching Walker acted again and again as examiner for the musical degrees. To this work he gave the same meticulous care and attention as he did to all his other work, and his insistence sometimes caused some irritation to his fellow examiners, especially to Parry.

I only met Sir Hubert once, when I sat next to him at a small party; he came in after we had begun dinner descending upon us like a whirlwind. He had been detained, examining students, and he blustered out 'it was a dreadful thing to do, examining all day, and Ernest Walker was there, insisting that enough time must be given to each candidate. Every one of them should be asked for a scale first, to settle in nerves and so on—he is quite right about it,' Parry added, with a smile, 'but heavens the fag for the examiner.'

Years later I discovered that Walker was generally known for avoiding the scamping of fag; he was consistently true to his own standard, and struggled as much as possible against mechanical marking and mass work. In an examination he would always collect the rough notes as well as the papers in case they might cast light on the candidates' ideas.

Many University examiners were content to take problems from some out-of-the-way published work hoping the candidate would not recognize them. But Walker countered this way of doing things wherever he could and in his own setting of advanced contrapuntal and harmonic problems he invariably composed all details himself; he realized that the candidate would be hampered if he knew the work and tried to avoid following it; and supposing he should fill in the original solution, how was an examiner to mark that?

Something may be said here about Walker's examining work outside the University. As has been seen, Farmer

had introduced him to examining and inspection in girls'
schools. After Farmer's death in 1901, the Girls' Public
Day School Trust formed a Music Advisory Board to carry
on the work of inspection. The Clergy Daughters' School
at Casterton continued under Walker the annual inspection
Farmer had begun. Often, after examining from 9 to 12.30,
Walker would play to the girls for half an hour before lunch,
increasing their opportunities of hearing and knowing good
music. One headmistress wrote to the Council about
Walker's unforgettable kindness to the children. Another
headmistress told of her dread of the music examination for
a highly strung girl, and how Walker had chatted for ten
minutes till all nervous strain had been forgotten and the
honours that were deserved were gained.

It used to be said that Walker knew more about the
girls' schools of the country than any man living. In an
Oxford 'Locals' paper that he was correcting he found to
his delight the pleasing remark 'Haydn thought Beethoven
a gruesome pupil because he was always asking why'—but
(as a fact) he himself welcomed a pupil's why. His plan
of teaching pupils together added zest to discussion
and he would group them in twos and threes, or take them
alone, as he thought best for them, completely prodigal
of his own time.

He also examined for the University of Birmingham and
elsewhere. When Donald Tovey became Reid Professor of
Music at Edinburgh in 1914 he wrote to ask Walker to
assist him as external examiner for the musical degrees:

It would be the greatest possible help and relief to me if you could
do this; I don't like the plan by which the professor does it all him-

self and examines his own pupils and you are the only man I can think of who has the necessary independence of English Musical Vested Interests.

In a later letter Tovey sketches what he wishes to do:

There are features I wish to get rid of sooner or later; they may be all classed as superfluous turnstiles. The *Rhetoric and English Literature* paper is a poor affair, and I hope I should be ploughed in *Acoustics* and *Vocal Physiology* on both of which subjects I am discoursing quite glibly. Also the Preliminary (which doesn't concern us here) exacts two modern languages in all cases—which seems to me to discourage that desirable character the musician who is interested in 'classics' of which there *are* cases!

The result was acceptance and many happy visits to Edinburgh. Walker discovered the manuscript of the Lyke Wake Dirge, haphazardly left among music on the shelves at the Toveys' house in Royal Terrace. He saw in it one of Toveys' masterpieces and insisted on having it sent to the Oxford University Press. His enthusiasm infected my family and led to its first hearing at our house when Donald was in Oxford for his Romanes Lecture.

Soon after Sir Hugh Allen went to the Royal College of Music as Director, he invited Walker to be the external examiner for the annual pianoforte competition. By this time Walker had developed a considerable technique in arriving at a verdict, marking under definite headings, for pedalling, for touch, for accuracy, for rhythm, and so on, and last, but not least, for general impression. It was always intelligent sensitive playing that he chose for distinction; mere brilliance, however flashing, had little chance with him. And there were, in consequence, surprises in the awards. Sir Hugh, as a rule, agreed with Walker's verdict, and characteristically applauded an examiner 'who took a great deal of trouble and did not care a damn for what others might say!' After Sir Hugh's resignation when Sir George Dyson offered the awarding of the big prizes, Walker refused reappointment. He dreaded he might be too tired, after a long day of listening to candidates playing, to read through the manuscripts and scores which were included in the competition for the Leverhulme Prize. Weighing the relative merits of a solo flute or a conductor against the claims of a thesis or composition seemed to Walker too much to ask of any examiner. There was no one to check decisions, and great fatigue induced a yearning for sleep.

Years later Walker often surprised and delighted performers at the Oxford Ladies Musical Concerts and similar events, by calling to mind details of the occasion when they gained the Hopkins or Chappell, or Blumenthal or Challen prizes, or the Clementi Exhibition or Leverhulme Scholarship. He might remember what compositions had been played and other details, and the artists would enjoy having their reminiscences refreshed.

Examining thus played a large part in Walker's life and took up much of his time. It involved drudgery of course, but the genuine interest which he took in the individual candidates—especially when the examination included interviews and not merely paper work—often converted it into pleasure.

4. Oxford and Elsewhere
1900–1925

THESE twenty-five years were perhaps the high-water mark of Ernest Walker's career. He was now a Doctor of Music and had an ever-growing fame as pianist, composer, and writer on musical subjects. Balliol after Farmer's death had appointed him as Organist and Director of Music, and he was raising the standard and the reputation of the Sunday Concerts. They were years full of work and responsibility and of genuine happiness for himself.

One significant change took place very soon in his domestic habits. In 1901 his father died and it was an obvious duty then to found a home for his mother. The lodgings in 15 Ship Street were given up and the lease of a house was bought. The isolation of the Anerley home became a thing of the past; 28 St. Margaret's Road provided scope for Mrs. Walker's occupations and a place where Ernest lived his own life as far as work and interests were concerned.

He had great respect for the personality of others and no wish to interfere in a sphere that was not his. He and his mother had few interests in common but his amiability made the household a happy one. The quiet understanding that had existed between father and son had been more intimate and complete. Mrs. Walker enjoyed giving tea-parties and oyster-patty lunches to undergraduates; her taste dictated the arrangement of the house and its furnishing, and with great optimism she dismissed her companions and maids and found new ones. Shortly before her death in 1910 she welcomed a niece from New Zealand, Ida Cooper, who shared the home for some time. Many friends will re- call Walker's study at the back of the house, the big Bech- stein Grand, the tidy writing-table in the window that looked out on the garden, the shelves with double rows of books, the arm-chair, and the welcoming gesture beckoning a caller to a seat. Often on the hearth-rug, sometimes oust- ing him from his own easy chair, Nigger and Peter would lie asleep, paw in paw, merged into one indistinguishable mass of sleek black cat-fur. Life that had always been most vivid for Ernest in things of the spirit became even more completely centred upon them. A quiet routine was con- genial and he exercised self-discipline in undertaking no more than he could manage without a sense of being driven.

To fulfil his daily duties as organist of Balliol he worked out the exact time for the morning walk to play at the eight o'clock Chapel service. Arrangements for the weekly Sun- day evening concerts were made with all his care for detail, the timing, the correct printing of programmes, the artists' travel and reception. The Balliol Concerts had acquired their reputation for distinction and meant much not only for the college and the University, but for the artists who played and for music-lovers in Oxford and beyond it. There must have been hardiness in Ernest Walker as well as wise management of health for, in thirty-eight years of service for Balliol, he only cancelled his own co-operation at one Sunday concert. On that occasion he asked me to accompany Erna Schulz's violin.

After Jowett's death there was no longer the impressive sight of the Master's procession at the beginning of a concert. Caird, who succeeded Jowett, was not himself musical, but his keen intellectual intuition enabled him to value music as one approach to truth and he would say that without understanding it, he could realize what was happening when great music was performed. Strachan-Davidson, who followed Caird in 1905, also realized the importance of the concerts and not infrequently came himself, especially if there were some work by Mozart or Haydn on the programme and he could follow the tune of a 'pleasing jig'. His death in 1916 was a great loss not only to Walker personally but to his work. Neither A. L. Smith nor his family cared for music and they hardly ever appeared at the concerts. The majority of the Senior Common Room were keen supporters and would troop in just before the concert began and occupy the seats reserved for them in the front. The Hall meanwhile was packed with undergraduates from all over the University and other guests, and often even the window-sills were used as impromptu seats. Walker's direction had raised the Balliol Concerts to the position of one of the great events of the week.

The Musical Society was well supported financially by members of the college and some generous gifts from outside, and this gave Walker the chance of engaging many of the famous artists whom he had come across at concerts in London and elsewhere, many of them feeling that—even if the fees were slender—an appearance at Balliol was a privilege. He was also always ready to give a chance to a young artist starting on his career, and many afterwards famous made their début at Balliol. It would be tedious to attempt to name those who took part in the concerts during Walker's régime, but the mention of even a few introduces one at once to a wide world of music. Among singers there were Plunket Greene, David Bispham, Gervase Elwes, Campbell McInnes, Steuart Wilson, Marie Fillunger, and Dorothy Silk; pianists included Fanny Davies, Leonard Borwick, and Donald Tovey; and instrumentalists Robert Hausmann, Adolf Busch, Marie Soldat, Adila and Jelly d'Aranyi, Alfred Gibson, and Lionel Tertis.

One outstanding concert, though it strictly belongs to an earlier period, must be mentioned here. On 8 March 1896 Joseph Joachim played at Balliol. Once before at a Sheldonian Concert Ernest had accompanied him in Tartini's Devil's Trill; now Ernest was on the crest of his form. The review spoke of 'Joachim's incomparable verve and insight which seemed contagious to his fellow-performers, especially was this true of Mr. Walker'. But more valued were the words reported by his nephew Harold, which Ernest wrote on a slip of paper. In answer to someone's remark that he had never heard him play the G major Brahms more beautifully, old Joachim had said, 'Yes, but then look how the piano part was played'. In 1948 this slip dropped out of an old letter I myself was reading to Dr. Walker; Joachim had written to him in appreciation of the sonata performance and ended his note 'and your accompaniment of the Hungarian Dances could not have been more perfect, as I felt I could do just as I liked'. Walker's face glowed with pleasure and modest pride as he recalled this concert more than fifty years later.

The affairs of the Musical Society were administered by an undergraduate committee with a don as Chairman. During the whole of Walker's time the Chairman was A. W. Pickard-Cambridge; among the many successive secretaries was William Temple. The committee were responsible for finance and general arrangements, and often at its meetings the members would make suggestions as to artists and music, but it was an understood thing that the final choice rested entirely with the Director. An inspection of the programmes of the twenty-five years would show how incomparably well he performed his task.

So within the scope of what the Society could afford his judgement was unhampered. It was difficult to get artists to give time for special study for Balliol Concerts, and the choice of items for the programmes had to be restricted, in most cases, to their existing repertoire. Still a wide range of composers was drawn upon. By his own performance Walker secured the first public hearing in England of Brahms op. 117 and the E flat Rhapsody, op. 119, and Scriabine's pianoforte solos and some Debussy. His rendering of *La Cathédrale engloutie* soon after its publication was remembered for its sensitive pianism and imaginativeness.

Walker enjoyed occasionally stealing, by twenty-four hours, a friendly march on the Monday 'Pops'. The Press gave credit to London as the Balliol Invitation Concerts usually admitted no reporters, but those in the know were aware that Balliol had in fact got in first. Artists felt stimulated to offer out-of-the-way works: the César Franck Violin Sonata was played when hardly anyone knew it;

Bispham and Agnes Nicholls sang newly published Strauss, and Gervase Elwes introduced Josef Marx songs. Marie Fillunger sang the whole cantata of Bach 'Ich bin vergnügt', as likely as not a first performance in England; Walker's rendering of the C sharp minor Prelude of Rachmaninov, as well as Reger's 'Aus meinem Tagebuch' must have been among the first. Not infrequently he gave a performance of some new work, especially if it were by a member of the college.

It was a tradition that the concert should end with a hymn or chorale, sung by the audience. Walker would himself have wished to abandon it, but he found that feeling for its retention was strong and added on the programme the name of the composer of the tune, thus bringing it into line with the rest of the music performed.

Besides the professional artists there were in those years Balliol undergraduates of exceptional musical talent whom Walker asked from time to time to take part in the concerts. Many of them afterwards became known as performers, composers, or writers. Two stand out above the rest. F. S. Kelly was an Australian who had been educated at Eton and came up to Balliol in 1899 as the second Nettleship Scholar in Music. He was a great oarsman, rowed in the University boat and for Leander in the Grand Challenge Cup, and held the unique record of winning the Diamond Sculls three times. But music had the first place in his interest and he soon made his mark both as a pianist and a composer; his last published composition was an elegy for string orchestra dedicated to Rupert Brooke and composed in the trenches at Gallipoli. He was killed in France in 1916.

Walker had not only a great liking for him, but a strong belief in his promise for the future.

Of far more importance for Ernest Walker was the advent in 1894 of the first Nettleship Scholar, Donald Francis Tovey, who was to be his close friend till his death. The Scholarship had been founded as a memorial to Nettleship by his friends, with a view to giving a musician the opportunity of a University education; the Scholar was required to read for Honours in a Final Honour School. Tovey read for Greats and, like Walker himself, had a natural aptitude for philosophy. Just as Walker fell under the influence of Nettleship, so did Tovey under that of Edward Caird, the Master. Tovey's education had been private—his father was a former Eton master—and he was already a proficient pianist and had composed. Walker lost no time in making the new scholar's acquaintance. Tovey was lodged over the lecture room, on the first floor, in the corner of the front quad at Balliol. When Ernest climbed the stairs to pay his first call on the new Nettleship Scholar he had no idea what a happy surprise was in store for him; neither Parratt nor Farmer had proclaimed Tovey's gifts, and here was an undergraduate, steeped in the music that Ernest loved best, a ripe musician who had nothing in common with other undergraduates except his age. An artists' friendship that lasted a lifetime was then begun. Walker has given a living picture of Tovey in an obituary article written for the *Monthly Musical Record* and reprinted as a preface to the posthumous publication of Tovey's essays—an admirable description, giving a true and concise portrait of the man. Besides talk and music at Balliol there were visits to

Northlands, Tovey's home near Egham, when Tovey offered Walker a volume of the *Bach-Gesellschaft* as a bedside book. Once at Balliol when Tovey missed roll-call, Walker went up at about ten o'clock to see what had happened. He found him fast asleep with his bed strewn with *Bach-Gesellschaft* volumes. Work achieved and work planned formed the main substance of their talk and Walker was much interested in a treatise on Aesthetics that Tovey never finished and in compositions that remained fragments. The two friends had a high regard for and close knowledge of each other's works. Tovey dedicated his Balliol Dances for pianoforte duet to Ernest Walker and F. S. Kelly, inscribing Ernest's copy 'with Balliolesque admiration and affection'. But with Tovey's elusiveness and Walker's reserve there remained an element of aloofness.

A letter written to Walker by Tovey on the death of Walker's father in 1901 shows both his feeling and his shyness:

I hope you will let me offer you my deep sympathy; such as can come from one who has not as yet had any experience so great and sad.

I know, however, what my own father is to me, and believe that the more one is alive to such a loss the sooner the time will come when memory of what one has possessed and been influenced by, will prove a greater comfort than it ever was a grief: at least, if there is anything human and good in what people call time's remedies.

You would not like me to try and say more than is within my depth, so I will go no further now.

I wish Nettleship were alive to write to you. However you still have, more than most men, friends who have some of his power and sympathy; and you will have more help from them and from your own resources in supporting this than often falls to people at such times.

You must take this for a great deal more than its words are worth, or you will do me an injustice. It doesn't represent my sympathy, but I can't say the real things simply.

Another letter in 1902 asking for a testimonial illustrates Tovey's rather tortuous sense of humour:

Dear Walker,

Like the microcephalous (don't know how to spell it) kangaroo up a gum-tree that I am, I forgot to mention before that I should immensely value (as you well know without my mentioning it but might draw the wrong inference from my not so doing) your moral and material support in the shape of a testimonial from you as representing the musical authority both of your musicianship intrinsically and of our College, in the matter of this London Professorship for which I, with no prospect of the getting thereof but simply and solely with a view of bringing myself before the Powers that Be as one that seeks things of the kind and would like that fact known in case something ever at any future period however remote might turn up, am standing.

(This would make a beautiful sentence translated into German with all the verbs at the end in ascending order of importance.)

If you could be an angel and give me a word (at Englefield Green) that I could send to the people so that they got it on Friday morning I should be ever grateful.

I am ever yours,
D. F. T.

P.S. Please remember me very kindly to Mrs. Walker.

An article on the Art of Playing Beethoven on the Harmonium will follow shortly.

Walker replied with a brief testimonial, which shows his sense of Tovey's high achievement:

Apart from his very remarkable gifts as pianist and as composer, he possesses an all-round knowledge of music which is not only of immense range but also of the most exceptional depth and critical thoroughness; and he has further a great power of lucid and enthusiastic exposition. I find it in fact difficult to express in adequate words my opinion of his musical attainments.

Ernest Walker,
M.A. D.Mus. Oxon.
Director of Music,
Balliol College, Oxford.

Towards the end of 1912 a crisis occurred in Walker's life, which led to a change in his relation to the college. As has been seen in the diaries there had been a general broadening of religious ideas verging towards a pure spiritual theism. And later on, by imperceptible stages further mental development led to a settled outlook of philosophical, agnostic humanism. Nevertheless, he had not thought hitherto that there was any inconsistency in the performance of the duties of organist at the Chapel services by one who held his views. He regarded his duties as purely musical: 'I could not instruct choir-boys to repeat confessions and creeds decently and in order; still less could I consent to any fetters on word or action. But as it is, I have none but musical functions: and no constraint, direct or indirect, has ever been laid upon me.' But now the wife of a friend of his went so far as to accuse him of dishonesty. Walker's conscience was much disturbed, and he wrote to J. A. Smith, then Waynflete Professor of Philosophy and Fellow of Magdalen, to ask his advice. Smith entered with sympathy into the doubts and scruples that were worrying

Walker. In a characteristic letter he gives a considered opinion:

As I understand, no conditions of any profession of belief are attached to your holding the position of organist, nor can your opinions in any way affect the proper fulfilment of your duties. That being so, I think no obligation rests upon you to make an unasked disclosure of them, or indeed to do otherwise than to decline to enter upon discussion of them unless it was made an express condition. The matter is thus in my view one solely for your own decision and it is a question as you say of what your conscience will stand. I think it would be different if you engaged in any overt propaganda, but that is not the case.

Saying he did not think that there could be any objection to his continuing and that the friends whose opinion should be respected would share this view, he adds:

Whichever way you decide I should think equally consistent with honour and honesty. . . . *More* than a conscientious decision no one has any right to ask for, and that I know you have made. I see no reason why you should alter it. I should almost go further. You are happily able to make your choice without the intrusion of pecuniary interests or family responsibilities. Others may not be so fortunately placed. To decide otherwise might, in spite of the sacrifice, involve a certain flavour of self-indulgence and so unfairly add to the burden upon the consciences of others. It is perhaps easier for me now to put these considerations before you just because I myself have in late years moved away from old ground to a position where I feel less repugnance to conformity and co-operation with those who are more conservative than myself. I am no longer so irritated or alienated by differences, so to speak, of dialect, and certainly I feel much less inclined to criticize conventional or antiquated forms. It is not that I can personally make much use of them but that I am more tolerant of differences of expression. Thus to myself the question of compromise is no longer so pressing and I am not so ready as of old to suspect dishonesty in others.

That is enough about myself. I have said so much because in a certain way I feel I may give slightly more weight to my opinion.

Ernest Walker's answer to J. A. Smith's argument could be found in his essay on 'Free Thought and the Musician': 'We need not be over-pedantically anxious to clear our lips of convenient and now conventionally meaningless forms of speech. But the proviso is that we must (and it is not always so very easy) make perfectly sure that these forms of speech really do not mean anything to anybody.'

Walker decided that he could not continue in an ambiguous position and in January 1913 he wrote to the Master, Strachan-Davidson, resigning the organistship: 'my only reason being that I have come to the conclusion that my religious opinions are not compatible with the discharge of the Chapel duties'. He at the same time expressed the hope that he might retain the direction of the concerts. The College accepted his resignation with great regret. The Master wrote:

I associate myself heartily with the Fellows in regretting the loosening in any way of the ties which connect you with the College and its music—but if it must be so, it must. Meanwhile I hope that you will hold fast to the care of the Sunday concerts and the general supervision of musical studies in this College with the title of 'Director of Music'. . . . We all feel that the College owes you much for all the care you have bestowed on its interests in this matter, both before and after Farmer's death, and hope that you may long continue to help us.

An undergraduate, N. F. Smith, took over the duty of playing in Chapel, and since that time the College has always appointed an undergraduate organist. The resignation had been a great wrench to Walker and involved some financial loss, but he was helped by the understanding sympathy of the Master and Fellows, especially of the chaplain, the Rev. H. H. Gibbon.

After the first war the Musical Society decided to pay full fees for the sake of the artists and because it was felt to be unfair to those who promoted concerts in the town to ask the artists to perform for a lesser sum at Balliol.

This decision was far-reaching. In earlier days great artists had played for the privilege and a pittance; a less personal approach to them was adopted now. But Walker agreed that the decision was right.

The war over, the concerts resumed their old character and vigour, and Walker threw himself into their revival with all his old enthusiasm. In May 1925 after twenty-five years' service as Director of Music and thirty-eight since he first took part in the college concerts, Walker felt that he wished to devote himself more to his work as a composer and writer, and wrote to the Master, then A. D. Lindsay, to resign his official position:

I shall hope always to retain my personal connexion with Balliol, and shall always be glad, if it should be wished, to take part in its music: but I should like to return to the irresponsibilities of the earliest of my thirty-eight years of College life.

Walker wrote personal letters to all artists who had helped in his concerts. Their answers were among the letters and reviews I read to him in his old age, when we substituted reminiscences for backgammon in the last half-hour before bedtime. These replies reflect 'dismay' and 'concern'. A few quotations from them will show the estimation in which he was held. Myra Hess condoled 'with Balliol and all artists who have performed there under your care. You always made it so enjoyable.'

Cedric Glover wrote:

Norman Smith was with me when I heard of your resignation, we were both quite stunned and had always thought of you as there for ever. I am afraid it will be a sad blow for the College music, your position was so emphatically a personal matter—had it not been for your friends and connections with the outside world there could have been no Balliol concerts.

One of his oldest friends Cecilia Gates said:

Thank you for writing yourself and not letting me hear this in a roundabout way. I don't think I would have believed it. I am sad about it—remembering away back so many years to good old John Farmer's time, with his pride in you and chaff over 'Walkerisms' and the 'Gabri' evenings and your viola variations and other count-less lovely times. For all these warm thanks and gratitude.

From Dorothea Webb:

I felt we had never had a more perfect ensemble. It made me feel completely at my ease. Thank you also for the careful rehearsing; every little detail you noted and remembered.

Norah Dawnay looked upon her singing at Balliol as 'the pleasantest in her life'.

Walker drew up a synopsis of his programmes, and had it bound for the College Library.

The Master and Fellows presented him with a small replica of the silver tankard given to the college by Kyrle, the philanthropist, known as the Man of Ross. It bears a Latin inscription:

Ernesto Walker

Per XXXVIII annos

Musicae artis apud Balliolenses

duci et fautori

d. d.

Magister et Socii

MCMXXV

It was probably the most prized of all his possessions.

A year later he was elected Honorary Fellow. This distinction 'thrust upon the most modest of men gave general satisfaction'. A deep debt of gratitude for his Balliol Concerts was felt far beyond the wide circle of acquaintances; three from among many letters show that his friends were gratified. From a colleague in Balliol:

I feel I must just write you a line to say that it is a great joy to me to think that you will have this new link of connection to the College, which owes you so much. For myself I like to think that our friendship over all these years has got—though it did not need it—a new bond.

Hadow, now Vice-Chancellor of Sheffield, wrote:

All heartiest congratulations. I am delighted not only to see an old friend honoured, but to see Oxford Music and English Music honoured in his person. Of all distinctions I think that an Honorary Fellowship is the pleasantest—others mean recognition of work, but this means friendship in addition. May you have many years in which to enjoy it.

And J. A. Smith:

I am delighted to see the news in today's *Times* that Balliol has added you to the list of its Hon. Fellows. No one in that list has better deserved his election. It will be a source of pleasure to your numerous friends here and elsewhere that your long service to the College and to the University and to Music have been recognized by those among whom your work has chiefly been done.

And so at the age of fifty-five Ernest Walker had resigned; it was the close of a chapter.

Yet at the time of life when many lyrical poets cease to feel inspiration, Ernest Walker was to develop a new and more intensely personal style.

5. Later Years

ERNEST Walker lived for over twenty years after his resignation from the Directorship at Balliol. He was often in college and might be found writing letters in the Senior Common Room in the morning or talking to a friend in the quad. The direction of the concerts passed first to Dr. W. H. Harris, and afterwards, when he became Organist at St. George's, Windsor, to Dr. Dykes Bower and then to Dr. Thomas Armstrong, now Organist of Christ Church. Walker no longer took part in the concerts, except that he appeared at the thousandth concert in May 1936, when four of his Helicon songs were sung and he played the Bach C major Concerto with Victor Hely-Hutchinson.

Much of his other work in the University went on. He taught and examined as before, and was still a prominent member of the Board of Studies and later of the newly constituted Board of the Faculty of Music. On Walker's resignation from the latter Board in March 1946, Mr. Platnauer, its Chairman, wrote about 'the particular value and character of your work long recognized in places far from Oxford as well as in the University itself. The Board is aware, too, that this work was done to a large extent without any reward other than your knowledge of the progress of the students who profited from it.'

That his devotion to his pupils and his care for their subsequent careers was undiminished is shown by a letter written as late as March 1946 to a former pupil who asked for suggestions as to illustrations for a lecture on French music and particularly on Berlioz and Debussy. Walker's reply shows his care for detail and his infinite capacity for taking pains for others. A few sentences may be quoted:

The 'Scène aux Champs' is miles the finest thing in the *Fantastique*, but perhaps, for what I understand is a somewhat miscellaneous audience, it is long and somewhat stiffish. What about the Waltz? or is there perhaps a Toscanini record of the 'Queen Mab' Scherzo from *Romeo and Juliet*? That is something like! About Debussy *L'après midi* certainly: it is the only chance of showing his jewelled scoring.

About the piano pieces—I should suggest 'Les Collines d'Anacapri' rather than the somewhat vague West Wind thing; and I should certainly substitute the magnificent 'Cathédrale engloutie' for the 'Voiles' unless you use it as an example for a composer's collapse.

Outside Oxford Walker to some extent pulled in his horns. Work for the Girls' Public Day School Trust had been given up in 1924; he now no longer sought engagements in London or elsewhere and he chose sparingly among much examining that was offered. The Royal College of Music he retained and he gave much time to writing and composition.

The friendship with my family began in 1900 when my sister went to college. She was drawn into musical activities by Rosamund Gotch and Mary Venables, and Ernest Walker sent tickets for Balliol Concerts. Before long we timed our visits to Oxford to fit in with special Balliol programmes; by 1911 a great friendship had been established with my father and mother, and Ernest was adopted, as

Marie Soldat and Donald Tovey and others had been, on terms of a quasi-member of the family: someone for whom our home was always open and whose interests could command our co-operation whenever we could be of use. Our move from Cambridge Gate to Gunfield, Norham Gardens, Oxford in 1916 closed down one of his London quarters, but Balliol rehearsals and hospitality for Balliol artists frequently came our way, and our music room continued to be the setting of many of Ernest Walker's and Donald Tovey's activities. Our house was the scene of much music-making, not a little of it memorable.

The first manuscript performance of the Organ Preludes, 'hot from the furnace' was given by Dr. Dykes Bower in New College Chapel as the climax to a 'Gunfield Choir' outing. The occasion was homely but the music was played with insight, sympathy, and mastery, and Walker, much gratified, had the pleasure of discussing technical details with the exponent.

During his stay at Christ Church Professor Albert Einstein came to us now and again to play string quartets with Marie Soldat, Margaret Reid, and Arthur Williams, or sonatas with Walker or me. Once he asked for our 'Schweitzer' performance and laughingly called out 'Black Schumann' where 'Strange Lands and People' is quoted from Schumann's Childhood Scenes, in the duet that Walker composed to greet me on my return from Lambaréné, where I had been at Dr. Schweitzer's hospital as a nurse. Performances of Ernest Walker's African Fantasia Duet were undertaken for the benefit of Schweitzer's hospital, occasions when Gabon crafts and my film of Lambaréné were shown. We established a tradition of an 'African party' given each year for Lady Margaret Hall freshers, in whom Walker always became interested. Schweitzer himself came to one of these parties and took pleasure in identifying the negro tunes and adopting, as he said, all our young guests 'as temporary nieces'. But the *Fantasia* and film recitals became too frequent when Women's Institutes also wanted them. To enable me to fulfil engagements without his own co-operation for the bass of the duet, Walker composed a piano solo *Fantasietta* on the same tunes. It was a pleasant surprise to him and us in 1948 that West African students had been delighted to hear their own tunes interwoven with Western music at a Denman College course. Mrs. Doherty from Nigeria and others, and later Mrs. Williams from Freetown, Sierra Leone showed special interest.

It was Ernest Walker's playing of Parry's *Shulebrede Priory Pieces* that prompted my mother to ask for piano pieces about us, and the outcome was 'Three Dedications' and 'Four Miniatures' and several piano duets, and the 'Easter Piece'; among them distinguished masterpieces and intimate lyrics, some only a page long but alive with fullness of thought and musical meaning.

The death of my mother in 1933 checked festivities then planned and came as a shock. Ernest Walker recorded his impressions of her in the *Oxford Magazine*:

Last Saturday should have seen the formal opening, by the Chancellor of the University, of the Deneke Building of Lady Margaret Hall; the ceremony was naturally cancelled owing to Mrs. Deneke's sudden death. The building was called after her, and for many years she had had, both directly and through her two daughters, very intimate links with the college. The annual Philip Maurice Deneke Lecture (founded in memory of her husband from the proceeds of their younger daughter's work) will, however, be given in the new hall on the evening of Tuesday next by Professor Einstein.

Born in Westphalia eighty-six years ago, Mrs. Deneke had had her home in England for nearly sixty, and in Oxford for seventeen years. In the prayer written for the funeral service, mention was made of her as one greatly endowed 'earnestly to follow after things beautiful and true', and thanks were given 'for her life among us, her strong purpose and courage, and her gracious gift of friendship'. She was indeed a notable personality; even casual acquaintances could not but be impressed by the blend of dignity and charm, seriousness and humour, and all of them somehow quite unlike anyone else's. She held to the old things, but did not let the new pass by unheeded; an ardent lover of poetry (especially Goethe and Wordsworth), of flowers, and, perhaps, most ardently of all, of music—with which her contacts had always been very intimate—she retained unimpaired to the end all her vivid interests and eager alertness, and also her gifts of subtly delicate manual craftsmanship. She touched life finely at many points, and those who were given the privilege of her friendship will feel that something very fragrant has become a memory.

After my mother's death my sister and I maintained with Dr. Walker the tradition of weekly meetings in term and regular migrations, three times a year, to the seaside cottage we had established in Southwold. It was near Hedenham, the Toveys' country house, and the frequent visits, and the music and reading that grew out of them, lent a sunset glow to a long friendship.

In 1939 when the prospect of billetees and protection in air raids presented anxious responsibilities, Walker was glad to join our household at Gunfield, and he entered into whatever was going on. He arranged Sixpenny Concerts with us to offer artists engagements, and he planned and wrote letters and played. He also offered help with the telephone (till then his bug-bear) and he lightened the work of household accounts as he had done in Southwold. He placed his scholarship at the disposal of others: large parcels of Mr. Fox-Strangways's translations would arrive, and Walker would spend hours with volumes of songs spread about him. He returned the manuscripts so fully dotted with suggestions that Mr. Fox-Strangways gratefully offered to publish his name as the co-translator. Walker discouraged that, but he was gratified that 'Kein Haus, Keine Heimath' (set by Brahms), which he had returned three times with fresh emendations, was in the end one of the best translations.

Then Mr. Hubert Foss brought about half a dozen suit-cases full of Donald Tovey's papers and Walker devoted hours with him, and many more alone, to sorting them for posthumous publication by the Oxford University Press.

In 1943 Dr. and Mrs. Percy Scholes settled temporarily in Oxford where they continued their work on the *Mirror of Music*. Discussions of music and other matters had long years before been reflected in the pages of Dr. Scholes's paper the *Music Student*, and parcels of the typescript of the *Oxford Companion to Music* had found their way from Switzerland to Southwold as well as to 28 St. Margaret's Road. Now frequent friendly meetings and stimulating talk were much enjoyed. File by file the *Mirror of Music* was read and afterwards, at Dr. Walker's request, the two published volumes were left permanently for light reading on the round table by his arm-chair. Dr. Scholes's interest in the reprint of Ernest Walker's essays, 1946, was invigorating.

Our Friday Club for undergraduates was an effort to let the gap be felt less that was caused by the closing of the Oxford University Musical Club and Union. There was tea and technical talk and young composers felt 'encouraged by Walker's praise and humbled by his complete lack of condescension'. The Club led to friendship with Geoffrey Bush, Bruce Montgomery, Christopher Longuet-Higgins, and many others. Later, concerts for soldiers in our music room, notably eighty given for the University Leave Courses, offered opportunities for touch with local talent and with soldiers. There was little that Walker did not try to do for the musical men who were off to the front; letters at Christmas 1948 showed how very many had valued his sympathy.

Whenever possible we had an hour of quiet music for our own enjoyment. By persisting we finished all Bach's Cantatas, playing on two pianos when we possessed a second copy and mingling hands on one keyboard for the others. Walker called to mind with pleasure other private musicmaking. He had joined informal performances of Bach Cantatas and other music with a group of friends that Mrs. Lane Poole and Miss Mabel Price called together. Ernest Walker and H. P. Allen accompanied at two pianos from *Bach-Gesellschaft* scores. Much ground was covered in a very enjoyable manner and the sessions always ended with the singing of 'Jesu, Joy of Man's Desiring' which at that time was hardly ever heard, and for which Robert Bridges had translated the text.

Between A.R.P. duties and amateur farm work I snatched many happy hours with Ernest Walker and Paul Benecke, playing all Haydn's Quartets, and many others, on two pianos, Walker leading with the first violin and viola from the score; the 'cello and second violin, from parts, were put in on the second piano. Now and again friends dropped in to take a hand and share our fun; especially Kitty and Philip Taylor, Tom Armstrong and Ken Andrews, and John Hough.

For the last twenty months of his life illness cut Walker off from playing. His courage was stoic, he never once uttered a complaint; he knew we missed his playing but nothing was said. He silenced the proffered sympathy of an old pupil, answering that life had been happy for him: he had no regrets, health had been good, and he had enjoyed many great friendships. He went on listening to music with unchanged zest; the broadcast of a new composition by a pupil or friend always found entry in his diary. On occasions both his wireless sets were tuned to allow quick transit from one orchestral concert to another, and he tried, score in hand, to follow minutiae of differing versions, and on one evening wedged in a string quartet 'just to hear the lovely Adagio again'. For a time he kept up the tradition of reading aloud to us; his mind and memory remained unimpaired. Old friends, artists, pupils, colleagues, composers dropped in to see him and gave him music or news or technical talk, and he let nothing fail that was done to give him pleasure.

On Sunday evening, 20 February 1949, the Balliol Concert party before their performance played to him his varia-

In Southwold, 1939

At the piano, 1938

ERNEST WALKER
Drawing by Sir Muirhead Bone, 1946

tions for left-hand piano, clarinet, and string trio composed at Paul Wittgenstein's suggestion, 1933. Ernest was with us at our eight o'clock breakfast the next morning—he had not had breakfast in bed since 1892—and after lunch he was dozing by the dining-room fire. Our grey cat, his valued friend, was rubbing against his chair, purring and demanding her usual petting; but she was asking in vain. Unexpectedly, in gentleness, he had been called to face the incommensurable things that he had struggled so hard to understand. In him the light of truth had not lacked the warmth of desire and now he had entered the next scene.

The flag at half-mast at Balliol told many the news, and we who had cared for him struggled with our own deep sense of loss and an awed gratitude for the fitting end. In *The Times* we read Dr. Thomas Wood's letter:

He was, perhaps, most like himself in the golden days of 1914, when all musical Oxford crowded Balliol Hall on Sunday nights for the concerts he directed there, and when he played on Tuesdays inimitably at the Musical Club. Then his beard was brown and his shoulders broad; he lived in St. Margaret's Road in a house that was neat to the point of primness where he could be called on at any time by any young man who wanted help in any matter that had to do with music. Beethoven to Brahms—that was his field; no-one we had ever met in those days knew it as well as he; and we found him so much at ease with the lives of the great composers that we felt (though we were very young then and he seemed old) that he must have been friends with all of them in turn. To examine with him in the Schools, twenty years later, was again to admire his range of knowledge; to listen as he came to an opinion was to learn what clear thinking can be. Though a kindliness that was innate fought hard with this. He was quite incapable of hurting anybody's feelings; and his anxiety on the one hand to let down lightly and his instinct for precision on the other would bring about a battle that was settled—as often as not—by one of those cascading shouts of laughter that were the delight of all who knew him. It meant an armistice had been signed. But if shoddy workmanship were in question, or wrong values—never an armistice then.

Of his own work and achievements he would say little. He was content that they should speak for themselves, as he was content that Oxford should be his world. And yet, when his friends went to visit him (as they always did) with news of the big world and with tales from the ends of it, he would question them eagerly, and astonish them by his knowledge of affairs as he had astonished them, years back, by his knowledge of music.

This alertness, this youth of mind, he kept to the end. Then the beard had gone white, and illness had made him a frail little figure (lovingly cared for) sitting in quiet. But it was still Ernest Walker. He was *sui generis*, but he was Oxford as well in his passion for beauty and truth.

Mr. Frank Howes spoke of Walker's influence being 'in the nature of a highly concentrated essence which from a quiet corner in Oxford pervaded wide areas of our musical life'.

Professor Westrup bore testimony to disinterested work as being 'more than is ever likely to be fully known or appreciated'.

Dr. Albert Schweitzer wrote from Günsbach, 'Now the dear, gentle, kind, distinguished Dr. Walker has left this life. Seeing him impressed me deeply each time. He belonged to the quiet, mysterious world which is closed to us men of common clay. How good that he fell asleep gently. But what a loss for you!'

6. The Musician

OF so many-sided a musician as Ernest Walker it is not easy to form a comprehensive judgement, and perhaps the fairest estimate can be reached by considering separately the various fields in which he worked.

Walker would never have claimed to be an organist. Indeed it has been seen that in early Balliol days he felt some difficulties in the management of the pedals. Yet many Balliol men remember the beauty of his playing of psalms and hymns and the varied charm of the voluntaries which often caused men to linger in the Chapel after the conclusion of the service. None of my family had heard Walker play for a service, but on the occasions of training the Lady Margaret Hall Choir for my father's funeral service, and later my mother's too, he offered help, and I realized his intense love for the beauty of the psalms and his originality and power in supporting them musically. The counterpoint he improvised around the chant put life into the whole choir. His Organ Preludes too testify to his full understanding of the capacities and characteristics of the instrument.

Much has been said already of Walker's reputation as a pianist and in particular as an accompanist, whether to voice or instrument. Here it is perhaps sufficient to add that his thorough musicianship, his careful study, and his natural sensitiveness made him equally at home through the whole range of music from Byrd to Bartok. But something must be said of his keen interest in the problems of the

technique of piano playing. The use of the pedal was the
subject of much inquiry and experiment, and after a recital
given in Oxford by Harold Bauer in 1911, the two musicians met and discussed harmonics and experimented on
Walker's piano. In a letter he wrote:

The astonishing thing was Bauer's series of secondary harmonics
—playing some harmonies and silently pressing down others that
would sound if their generators had been struck. Bauer played
Schumann's *Carnaval* and showed that in 'Reconnaissance' he could
take the repeated note with thumb and index finger while holding
on to the tune, and in the silent chord at the end of 'Paganini' he
struck the top note, almost inaudibly, to make it ring out after he
had pressed down the other notes noiselessly.

In writing to arrange their meeting (18 February 1911)
Harold Bauer mentioned his surmise that Walker had written the article on 'The Value of the Indistinct' in *The Times*
which he found so well expressed and so valuable that he
sent for a number of copies to distribute among his pupils.
Problems of this type had great attraction for Walker; he
himself had made much use of silent touch and kindred
effects and he experimented freely with 'definitely acous-
tical composition adventurings in unusual sound effects',
and in the last bar of Ravel's 'La Vallée des Cloches' he
found that 'an exquisitely ghostlike E major "harmonic"
chord is very unexpectedly, but quite clearly evocable'.
Walker said that lest he should be discouraged from continuing his practice of pressing down this chord silently,
he had cautiously refrained from confessing it to Ravel
when he met him on the occasion of his honorary doctorate in Oxford.

Nor were his inquiries always on this high level. A piece of original research that he delighted in was his discovery that Domenico Scarlatti's cat was either a kitten or an under-fed narrow-chested animal. His own corpulent Nigger and Peter could not walk along the keyboard striking two black notes in succession—whereas our kittens could easily paw the E flat to F sharp that occur in the theme of Scarlatti's Cat's Fugue. Now and again he would gently pick up one of our kittens; if it was in the mood (there was never any compelling), he would entertain the kitten, himself, and us by demonstrating his Scarlatti theory at the piano.

Walker's lasting appeal to those who did not know or hear him must be as a composer and a writer on musical subjects. His writings will be dealt with in the next chapter. Composition, as has been seen in the early diaries, was one of his activities from the first and it was continued right down to 1938. The majority of his work was vocal, or chamber music, but he occasionally made an excursion into orchestral music. Dr. Ivor Keys in the criticism quoted below, wishes that there had been more in this line, and it is interesting to find the same wish expressed in a letter from Donald Tovey written in 1931 after a performance of Walker's *Variations* at Edinburgh:

I meant to write long ago about your Variations which went very well in Edinburgh and made a decided impression, quiet though they are

What I chiefly want to say is that I *most decidedly wish you would write more for orchestra.* I'm beginning to consider myself fairly experienced as a judge of orchestration, and I don't think I can be

mistaken in seeing decisive evidence that you have natural gifts
therein which have survived a starvation that would have killed
anything killable.

Your orchestration is emphatically the genuine article. Do try something on a larger scale—preferably *not* with three-ply wind because
I can't afford extras except when the moon is Reckitt's blue—but
symphonic or overturish. I am quite certain that the handling of
this medium will be a stimulus to your invention and that you have
no reason to fear that it will fail. It would seem impertinent to say
this to you if I didn't know that you have written very little for
orchestra and that you are conscious of not having much practical
experience. Just rely on your excellently accurate imagination and
kick up a jolly row with your next large work.

The Variations weren't easy, and the quality of tone was con-
spicuously beautiful all through—also the balance.

In speaking of his own methods of composition Walker
once said that among his father's books there was a small
old edition of Shelley containing some poems that are not
included as a rule in the collected works. In these usually
unpublished lyrics there were spaces in brackets for lines
that the poet had intended to add later, and where a rhyme
or adjective had not leapt to mind, a dash indicated a space
for it. Walker owned that this book influenced him much;
it seemed to cast a light on the curious manner in which the
creative and mechanical were closely allied. He added:

The more contrapuntal the work the less I can use the piano as
a stimulus. The Horn Quintet and the Rhapsody and Fugue were
entirely paper work.

He would use the piano fairly freely in the early stages
of a composition, often humming to himself till ideas
would begin to crystallize and loose ends would knot them-

selves by a process beyond explanation. The actual work was done in white heat and Walker could never recapture that mood or alter a finished work.

More definite views as to a composer's methods were explained by him in 1930. A questionary propounded on the basis of some pages in Mr. Frank Howes's book *The Borderland of Music and Psychology* was sent to twenty-three composers. Their answers were published and Walker was invited by the *Monthly Musical Record* to contribute to the symposium and to comment on it. The three questions were (1) What is inspiration? (2) How is it maintained through a long work? (3) Of what is the composer chiefly aware in the process of composition—the idea or the emotion he is trying to express, or the solution of the purely musical problems involved? Parts of Walker's article speak of his own methods of work.

(1) Believing neither in spontaneous generation nor in angelic messages, I seem necessarily to fall back on this: that inspiration 'occurs' whenever something that arrests attention is thrown up out of the ever-seething mass of a composer's musical memories. How much it is worth—there is the rub, of course. But the problem seems no more, and no less, difficult than that of explaining any other manifestation of personality. And when I say 'memories' I do not mean that every composer is a plagiarist (though indeed the ingenious Germans who live laborious days over *Quellen-forschung* seem well on their way to think so); all I mean is that not even the most ardent revolutionary can escape from the past that has made him. And about the 'inspiration v. hard work' problem, it seems to me that the composer must, from moment to moment, be his own sole judge; he alone can decide whether what has arrested his attention is, as it stands, adequate or not for its specific purpose. If he decides

to omit the hard work, he decides at his peril, of course; but it is at his peril that every creator decides everything.

(2) Here one has inevitably to be personal. I can only say for myself that for any composition, up to a quarter of an hour or so in uninterrupted duration, I prefer to have it complete in essentials, either in my head or in a kind of shorthand scrawl in a note-book, before I sit down to pen and ink and music paper and the settlement of details. And it is perhaps a corollary of this particular method that, when once I have finished doing what I can over a piece of work, I find it impossible at a later date to go back and revise.

(3) I said that I believed all that exists to be rightly examinable by philosophy; but mysticism (in the best sense of an often misused word) is a part of philosophy, and it is in that corner that the problems of artistic inspiration, as of human personality in general, seem to lie. In the meantime, every good metaphysician must hold that the search is more important than the solution; and all a composer can do is to try to ensure that what is thrown up out of the seething mass in his own brain is something hot, and something alive.

Dr. Ivor Keys has been good enough to contribute a detailed and technical criticism of Walker's work as a composer, which is printed as an appendix.

7. Writings, Interests, Characteristics

THE great bulk of Walker's writing was naturally on musical subjects. The main portion of it is contained in three books. In 1902 he was invited by Mr. Wakeling Dry to write *Beethoven* for the Masters of Music Series. The proposition was on so small a scale that the treatment of Beethoven's music had to be compressed. Nevertheless, the last chapter (about one-third of the whole book) gave some opportunity for personal outlook. The Press spoke of 'reverence for the stateliness, the calm beauty and strength of Beethoven' as an outstanding feature 'of a capital little book that is neither academic nor purely popular. Dr. Walker has in fact pulled off a complete success. It is written by a musician who not only knows his Beethoven and loves him, but has evidently nine-tenths of his music at his fingers' ends.'

Two years later, the Oxford University Press gave him a commission to write a *History of Music in England*. He asked to be allowed three years and during that time read a great deal at the British Museum, at Bodley, and in the Library at Christ Church. He referred to no work in the History that he had not read, and he verified every reference. The finished manuscript was delivered to the printer two months ahead of the time stipulated. The publication created a considerable stir and there were many discussions in the Press. The review in the *Literary*

Supplement of *The Times*, 2 January 1908 may be taken as typical:

At last there is a book worthy of the subject. The author is known, though not too widely, as a composer of originality and a musician of excellent all-round capacity and taste; in his former writings about music he has shown considerable literary skill, although he has seemed to err on the side of too vigorous denunciation of the accepted objects of the ordinary Englishman's worship. In this book he wields the rapier rather than the hammer. . . .

On the Madrigalean era he is at his best, and he brings to life for us the conditions in which music was performed at the time. . . . In this brilliant chapter the writer gets at the very heart of the form, yet in the elaborate and detailed explanations there is no trace of pedantry.

In some ways the chapter on 'Handel in England' is the best in the book. Dr. Walker is none of your iconoclasts who think it right to decry everything that Handel wrote; his position is well summed up in the words: 'No other composer can ever attempt to rival Handel in his power of intensely irritating those who have the strongest and sanest admiration of his genius; no one, it is true, is always at his best, but the pity is that Handel is so often at his worst. . . .' Dr. Walker writes so well and wisely, so thoroughly yet so concisely that the book deserves most hearty welcome. The whole outlook of the book is individual and appreciative, a scholarly work written more for musicians than for antiquarians and eminently readable.

A reprint was required in 1924, but it had to be made by a photographic process and Walker regretted that many modifications that seventeen years of experience suggested to him could not be introduced. One correction Walker would gladly have made.

Among the manuscripts of Samuel Wesley acquired by

the British Museum there were copies of pieces by Byrd with nothing to indicate they were not Wesley's own. Grove's *Dictionary* included them in the list of Wesley's works; Walker had the insight to recognize their Elizabethan style and to comment on it, but he was trapped into accepting them as Wesley's compositions and criticized them accordingly. A letter from H. B. Collins, of the Oratory Church, Birmingham, first pointed out the slip to him. It was unlucky that this letter came just too late to allow correction in the second edition. The Oxford Press would no doubt have reprinted that page.

Shortly after finishing the *History of Music*, in 1908 Walker was asked by Ernest Newman to write a volume for *The New Library of Music*. He reluctantly refused:

Shorter literary engagements like analytical programmes, revising articles in dictionaries and periodicals and so on, I would indeed be grateful to have more of: one can see the end of them at starting, and they have no drawbacks of any kind. But to have a lengthy book hanging over one's head for an indefinite but anyhow considerable period is to me somehow, I confess, a sheer physical torture that, on grounds which are virtually those of health, I feel bound to fight shy of unless either I have an urgent desire to express some (to my mind!) salutary doctrine or else the 'bread and butter' inducement is of a substantial nature. I am continually, like Io with her gadfly, feeling impelled to add to my already large stock of probably unsaleable compositions, and I somehow grudge giving my leisure hours to other things.

Walker's third book is a collection of essays reprinted in 1946, from *The Times*, the *Literary Supplement*, the *Manchester Guardian*, and other publications. He was severely self-critical and chose to have a small volume. The first essay which gave its title to the book *Free Thought and the Musician* will be mentioned later. Of the essays on musical topics Dr. Armstrong wrote in the *Musical Times* of March 1949: 'these articles are like Walker's talk and give a vivid impression. One sees the quick eager response, the slightly academic humour, the strong opinion backed with knowledge, experience, and memory. One notes the firmness where any matter of principle is involved, the generous admiration of other artists, the intolerance of humbug or pretension, however eminent the pretender.' Walker's style is moulded on the power and strength of biblical language and the rhythm of his sentences recalls his close intimacy with the Old and New Testaments. He was scrupulous in the choice of words and punctuation. And he had great variety. Always an inward vivacity is at work whether in closely packed analytical notes, or in compressed estimates, or in more expansive writing. His memory for detail is supported by imaginative experience and often opens up a wide vista of unusual features perceived. Then, too, he has a mastery in brief portraiture; he says much in very little and is wholly devoid of guff. His essays and reviews, mostly written for some immediate occasion, may well subsist by their intrinsic value and lasting interest for the quality of his criticism is creative.

The collection reprinted in 1946 can be regarded as an illustration of the many essays and reviews which Walker wrote for periodicals and magazines. He also contributed articles to Grove's *Dictionary of Music*, of which the most important are Oratorio, Debussy, and Degrees in Music.

Walker often responded to calls for analytical notes for concerts. There are programmes for Lawson's Classical Concerts, 1899, and Acott's series, as well as the B.B.C. Toscanini events (1938) and Oxford Musical Festivals, Kruse's Popular Concerts and Weingartner Festivals, the Classical Chamber Music Society, the 'Proms' and many others. Even in the restricted space of concert notes his humour and judgement may be seen and he hits many a nail on the head neatly. As a specimen of Walker's analytical notes may be taken his introduction to Elgar's *The Kingdom* written for the Leeds Festival in 1907. After explaining that this work was part of a large conception of the composer's, the first two sections of which were embodied in the earlier oratorio *The Apostles*, Walker continued:

The Kingdom is entirely taken up with the third portion of the scheme—the establishment of the early Church, in Jerusalem, on the spot intimately connected with its now invisible Founder. The salient features consequently are the works of fellowship of those who had personally known their Lord, and the outpouring of the promised gift of Pentecost; the whole atmosphere is one of young energy, illuminated from time to time by gleams of the formerly constant supernatural element, no longer primarily mystical, but rather the human energy of men who are putting their hands to the plain work that lies before them. And the music of *The Kingdom*, essentially (in its main outlines at any rate) more diatonic and direct than that of *The Apostles*, expresses the composer's ideas quite apart from his words: it is broader and more symmetrical in structure, and moves, not in a dim and only half-realized light, but in the full sunshine of day, the brightness of which is not clouded, but rather explained and justified, by the occasional glimpses of a further world, now better understood than before.

The writing of these notes was preceded by an amusing visit to Elgar, which Walker liked to relate. He had written to ask if there were any points which Elgar would wish emphasized and received an answer which, after some very technical details, invited him to come over and stay a night. Walker arrived in time for lunch, and in the afternoon the composer with Lady Elgar and their daughter took him a motor drive along the banks of the Wye. For tea they were back in the drawing-room, where rows of Elgar's works bound in white vellum, were prominent on the book-shelves, and presented an air of 'pomp and circumstance'. And on the staircase this was emphasized by enormous laurel wreaths that had been presented at German concerts, with golden letters on big coloured ribbons. A fresh-air saunter round the garden between tea and dinner was wel-come and Elgar explained, with nervous gestures, his experiments on Luther Burbank lines; the netted twigs and the strange fruit he had cultivated: a hybrid between an apple and a pear.

He spoke of his experiments in chemistry which the day before had caused an explosion; he had picked up some-thing that was on fire and had thrown it into the water-butt which, in protest, burst, setting free a big stream down the drive. After dinner Walker was taken to the study, a room that held a valuable heraldic library, works on chemistry, and no sign of music except one upright piano: Elgar said if he had been able to live a completely independent life he would have liked to be an M.P. Innocently Walker asked for which party: 'Conservative, of course' Elgar snapped out. Again a silence and again Walker tried to get conversation on to *The Kingdom*, but Elgar went to the piano and played from his own 'Wand of Youth', stopping now and again to say he would like to incorporate this or that musical idea in a bigger work. He also said he often worked at orchestral colour preparing his palette with effects of sound and combination of sound, independent of any composition, merely so as to have experiments ready at command if ever wanted.

At last towards the end of the evening Elgar spoke about his great cycle of oratorios, of which *The Kingdom* was one, and on this late conversation much of Walker's notes was based.

The essay on 'Free Thought and the Musician' must be considered separately, for it is an expression of Walker's deepest convictions: 'The great work of all the creators in the whole field of spirit has its roots far deeper than any spatial or temporal happenings, down in the mysticism, or whatever we like to call it by which we chiefly live.' It has been seen earlier how he veered away into agnosticism and then into atheistic rationalism, always retaining a sense of mysticism, closely connected with his love of nature. This led, as has been recounted, to his resignation from the post of Organist at Balliol. He now became more actively connected with the Rationalist movement, and when his mother's death in 1910 closed all personal claims, Walker began to reflect what good he might do posthumously by leaving his money to a cause he had at heart. He had thought of endowing a lectureship on Rationalism at one of the universities, but was discouraged by one of the leaders of the movement, who held that what was needed was a more popular appeal. Later he made a will in favour of Somerville College, though he regretted that it offered 'optional religious observances', but when in 1932 the College built a chapel for undenominational services, he reluctantly revoked his will, holding that 'undenominationalism is only one among other Christian denominations, and a rather specially illogical one'. Towards the end of his life in 1945 an old pupil asked him to be godfather to her child. Walker refused saying 'the office of godparent is to my mind an exceedingly serious religious duty, and I am not fitted for it'. In the essay itself Walker makes a reasoned plea for the freedom of the musician who cannot hold orthodox religious views, but with his usual scrupulous understanding of those who differ from him.

Walker was primarily and to the depths of his nature a musician, and other occupations made little appeal to him. But chess attracted him, as it has many other musicians. Even in his schooldays he played and some little grey notebooks with many reported games bear witness to his consuming interest. A typical entry may be chosen at random from the diaries: 'P. had two games with me, one Q.P. opening (I played black) the other a Centre-counter (white). Won both rather easily.' Walker never joined the Oxford University Chess Club but he was asked whether he might be available to play for the Club against Cambridge. Then he declined on account of work. Later on, about 1902, he took up chess more seriously. He did original research in the Max Lange opening and for a few years he met Professor Vinogradoff, E. I. Carlyle, and J. A. J. Drewitt regularly at the Vinogradoffs' house, or at Lin-

A musical conundrum sent to Trevor Harvey on a postcard, referring to B.B.C. performances of *England's Helicon* and *Say, Dainty Dames*

Balliol College Musical Society

A Concert in Memory of
ERNEST WALKER
(1870—1949)

HON. FELLOW OF BALLIOL COLLEGE

DIRECTOR OF THE BALLIOL COLLEGE CONCERTS

Balliol College Hall

Monday, May 23rd, 1949, at 9.0 p.m.

DOORS OPEN AT 8.45 P.M.

Cavatine, Adagio molto espressivo   *Beethoven*
     from Quartet in B flat, op. 130

Fantasia in D for String Quartet, op. 32 (1908) - *Ernest Walker*

Quartet in F, op. 135   -   -   -   *Beethoven*
     Allegretto
     Vivace
     Lento assai
     Grave—Allegro

Quartet in D (K. 575)   -   -   -   *Mozart*
     Allegretto
     Andante
     Menuetto. Allegretto
     Allegro

THE BUSCH QUARTET

ADOLF BUSCH   BRUNO STRAUMANN

HUGO GOTTESMANN   HERMAN BUSCH

Programme of first Memorial Concert, 1949

coln College. They each of them played two games at a
time. Walker also joined the City Club and won games for
them against Reading, Swindon, Cambridge, and Oxford
University. In a tournament when Blackburn took on
twenty-four players Walker drew his game. On another
occasion he saw Blackburn playing blindfold against eight
players. In conversation afterwards Blackburn seemed
quite unconscious of the astonishing feat he had performed
and said quite simply he could not understand how anyone
could play music by heart. Walker once witnessed the
rather dreadful sight of a big tournament in the Examination Schools. Most of the players were at the end of their
nerves and Atkins, the champion, was drinking one glass
of milk after the other, while another player kept his eyes
fixed on his little girl's photo with the words written on it
'Please play well Daddy'. About 1906 Ernest Walker was
playing for the Oxford City Club against Smith, the
amateur champion of England. The game went on for four
hours on end and reached a position which was a forced
draw. Walker was so tired that he missed the move and lost
the game. Afterwards he found himself playing the game
over in his sleep and, on his doctor's advice, he gave up
serious playing.

He was never proficient at outdoor games, but from his
undergraduate days he played lawn tennis—unscientific-
ally but with great enjoyment. Years later we played with
him on sea-side holidays—he was always winning by cutting and placing; our supposedly swift strokes had no
chance against him.

Cricket held a higher place; even in old age play in the

Parks attracted him. As a small boy he had accompanied his father, also keenly interested, to Crystal Palace matches and to Lords. His own school efforts reached a top score of four, but they acquired for him a quick eye for finer points in the game. Although excellent at dancing he was never keen.

His love of walking and the country never deserted him and in later years holidays—rarely longer than a fortnight—were spent visiting friends or enjoying the untrammelled freedom of travelling alone. His passion for nature and his interest in the details of architecture or art could absorb him completely. Naturally retiring he was inclined in conversation to leave initiative to others; he often came upon companionship and good talk on his journeys, but solitariness never bored him. Sometimes professional engagements presented a setting which he enjoyed. One exquisite Elizabethan house, of mellow red brick, gave opportunities for a visit to Salisbury Cathedral and walks in the New Forest; and there was a terraced garden near Bath with a grey sixteenth-century house that clung to the sloping side of a hill. Here the then fashionable C Sharp minor *Prelude* of Rachmaninov was in frequent request, but the more vivid memory was the adventure of stroking a bat, that clung to a ledge near the front door, fast asleep in the sunshine; and lying down to rest during a lonely walk, Ernest was entranced to see a weasel come out of her hole with several baby weasels and gambol about quite near his feet; another time a family in Surrey caused him to share their intimacy with wild red squirrels.

Once when Walker visited the Glebe Farm at Spelsbury, the owners asked him to name a calf just born—an Old

Testament name was obligatory. He was determined to do as well as he could and begged time for reflection. Back at Gunfield, he consulted his well-worn school Bible and turned up the 27th chapter of Numbers to search the list of daughters of Zelophehad. He had an idea that might be fruitful: he chose Milcah. Social entertainments, if not too frequent, had attraction for him; in a letter to me he speaks of 'a sardine-like squash, and I rather proud of my skill in bringing, without disaster, simultaneous cups of coffee to your sister and Miss Skipworth. But it is not disagreeable to have such opportunities of two-or-three minutes' talk with folk one otherwise seldom comes across.'

There were some fashionable engagements that Walker remembered with amusement; an At Home where the late King of Sweden sat in the front row conversing ceaselessly, and Walker's tactics to startle him into silence—alternate fortissimo and pianissimo bars—proved unavailing. Also an evening when the programme of music was dwarfed by a sumptuous banquet. Brandy from the time of Napoleon was served (all alcohol had evaporated), and Chateau Margot in precious bowls, with an environment of giant roses and stunted trees in Chinese vases.

But mostly he enjoyed being with his musical friends such as Rosamund Gotch, Mary Venables, Sylvia Farnell, or the Prices. Some happy holidays were spent in Scotland with the family of Dr. A. J. Carlyle; there were duets, chess, and talks on the classics with the family Lewis. He had a tender-hearted generosity in playing to those whom years or illness cut off from concerts, and he set aside regular dates for Miss Molyneux and Miss Sarah Acland. His old

friends, the Dennistons and Miss Una Goodwin introduced him to the pleasures of broadcast concerts. Much of
his spare time in term was spent with us; and vacations in
our Southwold cottage had fostered a sense of companionship that held good after our return to Oxford. So he all
but belonged to our Oxford household before Gunfield
became his permanent home in 1939. It had been impossible to live with him for years without becoming increas-
ingly aware that beneath his composure there was ardour in
restraint. He was remote from self-assertion and it needed
probing to discover his opinions but we grew hesitant about
disregarding them, for little escaped his notice and his
judgements were just and his standards fine. Those who
knew his gentleness and quietude realized above all the
purity of his spirit and the serenity of a conscience at peace.
He was inclined to believe the best of everyone and was
readier to excuse human mistakes than error in scholarship.
Donald Tovey described him as a 'spiritual disinfectant' for
sayings that were harsh or ugly did not get far with him;
by a remark, usually humorous, he would disclose fresh
aspects.

His puritan outlook made orderliness and punctuality
part of his being, but he wasted no comment on them.
Editors could rely on an article of the right length at the
promised time. Library books were returned punctually,
bills and taxes were paid by return of post, and a meal was
respected at its own hour. With a touch of austerity he
habitually copied into each new cheque book details that
might save his executors trouble. His word was his bond
and quite effortlessly he realized the point of view of others.

In politics he was a Liberal and only on two occasions did he show indignation. He was relentless about the miners' selfishness in the General Strike and complete in his condemnation of the gangster methods of suffragettes, perhaps the more so since he was a steady supporter of 'Votes for Women' from early days. There was great moral courage and, afraid of no one, he often championed minority views, opposing blood sports and cruelty in any form.

On hearing his own compositions Walker would feel astonished that it was he who had written them; he would seem so completely outside them. Writing informally in a letter he says:

Went to Cathedral yesterday evening to hear 'Lord Thou hast been our refuge': they do it every now and then there (only on Sunday evenings, so as to have full strength) but I have not heard it myself under Dr. Harris before. A fine dignified performance: Louis Smith as soloist extremely good. I suppose it is the most emotional thing I have written (it rather curls me up myself): no doubt that is why Walford Davies is so tremendously keen about it. Anyhow it (the first six and the ninth verses of Psalm 90—some of the rest isn't at all as fine) has always struck me as terrifically great poetry with its conception of spiritual refuge in the thought of unchangeableness, even though the Unchangeable obviously doesn't care a brass farthing for us. And what English those old people could write! 'Again thou sayest: come again ye children of men'—with the repetition of 'again'—superb!

For a thousand years in thy sight are but as yesterday: seeing that is past as a watch in the night.

As soon as thou scatterest them they are even as a sleep: and fade away suddenly like the grass.

In the morning it is green, and groweth up; but in the evening it is cut down, dried up and withered.

For when thou art angry all our days are gone: we bring our years to an end, as it were a tale that is told.

The words 'integrity' and 'sensitiveness' have often been applied to Walker both as a musician and as a man. The integrity which led him to choose the best music and be always true to his ideal was reflected in his life and in particular in his unswerving loyalty to his convictions. The sensitiveness which seemed to make him know by instinct the meaning and intentions of a composer, showed itself not in any sensitiveness for himself or for his own claims, but in a quick recognition of the feelings of others. The words inscribed on Nettleship's memorial in Balliol Chapel were implanted in his mind and were often on his lips. His own life seemed to echo them:

He loved great things and thought little of himself; desiring neither fame nor influence, he won the devotion of men and was a power in their lives; and seeking no disciples he taught to many the greatness of the world and of man's mind.

Ernest Walker as Composer

By IVOR KEYS

Such periodic appraisals of Walker's music as were made in his lifetime were almost unanimously approving, yet for various reasons it is still little known as a whole. An examination of some of these reasons throws interesting light both on the man and on his music.

In the first place he was of a retiring disposition. Although in his aesthetic judgements he could be outspoken in condemnation and praise (a reviewer of his article on 'Oratorio' in Grove called him 'an autocrat in carpet slippers'), he was in his music, except in moments of passion, quiet and fastidious. He was not a pusher of himself and addressed his music to him that had ears.

His style sprang from the German classics. Some writers, knowing that the recent English Renaissance has gone farthest on the impetus of folk-music and modalism, have been inclined for this reason to discount the value of Walker's work. Such criticism is confused; indeed recent trends, even if Walker had not followed them, would not have made his music either good or bad. But in point of fact he was not uninfluenced; for whilst his earlier work, such as the five songs from 'England's Helicon', is couched in diatonic language, about the middle of his career in 1914 he took to new harmonic paths, and such works as the two *Epitaphs* in op. 30 or the 'cello sonata could not even by the most casual hearer be labelled Brahmsian.

Much of the music is occasional, even private, composed for diverse combinations and circumstances. Walker had a craftsman's skill and pride. Time and again one sees the bold, even reckless, flight of fancy made coherent by artifice of counterpoint and harmony: and when the flight is short, the craftsmanship will seize on musical initials of friends, one-handed piano techniques, choirs of uncertain powers, five-finger exercises—and in the process make music. He had a great love of musical puzzles of all kinds and delighted in the abysses of harmony momentarily glimpsed, as often in Bach and late Beethoven, through some contrapuntal necessity.

The bulk of his work is small. Suffice it to say that there were many things to which he unstintingly gave his mind, especially his teaching of undergraduates. Teachers will know the constant study and ever deepening criticism of style—one's own included—which this work involves. There is evidence that Walker asked to be excused tasks well within his power in order to give more time to composition. But he must have thought that teaching could not thus be set aside. Whether this meant partial suicide as a composer we shall not know.

To his earlier period belong the works which are still the best known. They include the songs 'Corinna's going a-maying' and 'Bluebells from the clearings', the three-part songs 'Sister, awake' and 'Say, dainty dames' and the well-loved 'Five Songs from England's Helicon' for four voices and pianoforte. It is significant that these are all vocal works. Indeed, the *Fantasia* for string quartet excepted, the instrumental works of the period are burdened by the weight of their structures and lack the spontaneity of the songs. Colles's appreciation of his songs is as valid to-day as when he wrote in the third edition of Grove: 'He exhibits a vein of intimate feeling for the implications of English poetry and an instinct for apt musical expression which place him high among the song-writers of his generation.'

One means of learning his craft was by setting German words. Outstanding is Uhland's 'Frühlingsruhe', op. 1, the repose of its cadence hovering between genius and crudity. The best songs in op. 12 are Christina Rossetti's 'Dream Land', marked 'sempre pianissimo', and 'Some asked me where the rubies grew', an exact reproduction in music of Herrick's artful simplicity. Even the stodgy song of this group, Thomas Moore's 'Anacreontic Ode', derives its character from the words.

The songs in two and three parts, some of them written for school use and some for the Misses Eyre, whose pure matched voices delighted audiences of the time, show the same qualities as the solo songs. Musical sensitivity characterizes them, however humble the occasion or slight the probability of a wider hearing. In op. 7 craftsmanship and integrity are lavished on pieces which for all Walker knew would never go outside the schoolroom. The innocent freshness of Blake's 'The Echoing Green' can only be caught by a rapt performance: and a harassed schoolmistress will need to dedicate herself anew each time she sets her fingers to the limpid triplets evoked by 'the bells' cheerful sound'. Dedication is indeed always demanded, and painstaking effort to capture precisely the atmosphere required. Walker sometimes goes to almost humorous lengths of Italian in directions, asking the choir of the Clergy Daughters' School at Casterton to perform Shelley's 'Song of Proserpine' 'larghetto tranquillo ed un poco maestoso'. Of these ensemble pieces some depend on felicities of harmony and accompaniment, and some tend to relapse into thirds and sixths, a licence that trainers of youthful choirs will readily forgive for its sweet sound. The majority, however, could hardly be bettered, and 'Say, dainty dames' from op. 17 may well be technically the best thing Walker ever did, containing as it does featherweight counterpoint and buoyant and brilliant 'Fa-la' refrains which are a delight to sing and hear.

The other important vocal works of this earlier period are 'Five Songs from England's Helicon', op. 10, the 'Hymn to Dionysus', op. 13, the 'Ode to a Nightingale', op. 14, and the three songs, op. 27. 'Helicon' is as original and fresh as ever, except perhaps the third song, 'Love the only price of Love', which seems to have gone too far in matching the pompousness of the words, while the accompaniment suffers in comparison with its brilliant neighbours. Opp. 13 and 14 are both written for choir and orchestra: the orchestral writing, especially of the latter, is so obviously sure in obtaining beautiful and characteristic sounds that one can only deplore the absence of more orchestral music, for apart from the small-scale accompaniment of op. 38, and the 'Norfolk' Variations there is nothing else of importance. The 'Hymn to Dionysus' is a setting of a chorus from the *Bacchae* of Euripides. Gilbert Murray's flowing stanzas are set to music mainly tranquil; the melodies are distinguished if not outstandingly individual, and there are characteristic enharmonic modulations. This work is typical in its measured grace and lack of rhetoric; Walker is a quiet, fastidious Bacchanal.

The 'Ode to a Nightingale' is remarkable for the clarinet's song of full-throated ease and for the way the balance of the poem is maintained through the transitions between solo and chorus. An example of this kind of skill is seen where the chorus sing 'In faery lands forlorn'; 'forlorn' takes up the soloist like a sigh. Only an impeccable judgement could have handled this poem without degrading it. The harmony is tender with a lovely chain of modulations as the white hawthorn, fast-fading violets, and coming musk-rose unfold one after another. The unaccompanied, four-part op. 24, 'The splendour falls', contains one of the composer's most poignant cadences.

Two of the songs in op. 27 call for mention as they show a marked increase in the subtlety of the melodic declamation. They are 'In the spring twilight' and 'Snowdrops'. Both poems are by Sydney Dobell; they are not perhaps great as poetry but they have musical repetitions and symmetry which Walker found stimulating. The latter song has a characteristic melody consisting almost entirely of notes of equal length, and deriving its shape and its rhythms from the words, independent of metrical bar-rhythms.

The two fine anthems op. 16, 'I will lift up mine eyes' and 'Lord, Thou hast been our refuge', were originally scored for men's voices and organ, but Walker also set the second for mixed choir at the suggestion of Henry Ley. Its solemnity is striking; especially fine is the series of dark modulations beneath the central bass solo and the long silence before the last chord. Walker in revising the anthem for a reprint was determined not to modify this, and in any case he was never fond of afterthoughts.

The instrumental music of this earlier period is not as interesting as the vocal music. There are presages of a more adventurous style but the composer is preoccupied with the problems of construction. These few works are reminiscent of Brahms both in methods of development and in instrumental style; two works, however, must be excluded from this generalization: they are the Fantasia for string quartet, op. 32, and the Violin Sonata, op. 44. In both cases the number is misleading; the former was written in 1905 and published in 1923, and the latter dated 1910 was not published until 1930. The Fantasia is a work of charming, youthful grace. It opens with an Adagio, distinguished by the shapeliness of its lines and the subtlety of its spacing; this gives way to a Vivace, a shadow-play through which harmonics gleam; in the coda the material of the Adagio returns in reverse order with enhancement of feeling.

The violin sonata has some features which lift it well above the other early sonatas, notably the two fine bursts of passion, one in the peroration of the first movement and the other in the middle section of the slow movement. The variations which form the last movement have a lovely theme; it is the first sixteen bars of the Prelude in E flat for piano published as op. 37. This piano piece in fact dates back to 1904 when it appears in manuscript as the first and best of a suite called 'The Days of the Week'.

The year 1914 saw a sudden increase in harmonic subtlety. There are plenty of harmonic adventures before this date, but they are usually placed at strategic moments against a diatonic background, adding a sudden romantic depth, *à la* Haydn, to a coda, or momentarily entering a new world in the last stanza of a strophic song. But from 1914 the range of harmony becomes suddenly wider, scaffolding is dispensed with, and the style becomes more terse, allusive, and even enigmatic—the imagination is harder at work.

The most important work of this period and perhaps the pinnacle of Walker's achievement as a composer, is the Sonata in F minor for 'cello and piano, op. 41, but hardly less important for the history of his development are the two *Epitaphs* in op. 30.

In the 'cello sonata inhibitions have been swept aside by a torrent of passion which is almost unique in Walker's music. The old harmonic landmarks are submerged for long periods at a time, and now no part of a composition is necessarily stable in its key. In particular there is nothing in his work like the tempestuous development in the first movement. A pianist who thinks this over-stated should try sight-reading the first movement at the proper speed; he will discover the abrupt transitions of harmony soon enough, and be made to recognize here a new style that contradicts generalizations based on earlier works. There is nothing finer in the chamber music than this first movement and it is matched by a deeply calm Adagio. The last movement strikes a perfect balance between weight and levity.

At first glance the two *Epitaphs* for three unaccompanied voices are simple homophonic pieces. It is doubtful, however, whether they have received many good performances, for they suddenly and without the help of accompaniment plunge into enharmonic progressions dangerous to less than the highest skill. The composer is in fact beginning to treat chords as colourful entities in their own right. It was not for nothing that he steeped himself in Debussy.

The torrent of the 'cello sonata having both deepened and broadened the channel of Walker's thought, a new ease and adventure is found in the best of his subsequent work. There is little on a large scale, but a series of exquisitely turned miniatures whose subtlety of harmony reminds one of Fauré's later style. Indeed it may be legitimate to press the analogy a little closer. Both composers were born in a classical tradition of music, and as they wrote, upheld the standards of a culture that was dying round them. Both prized logic and clarity and enjoyed solving the age-old problem of crystallizing the outpourings of a wayward imagination.

The vocal works of this later period are short, with the exception of the motet 'One generation passeth away'. There are only two solo songs, op. 38, both to poems by Sydney Dobell—'Summer Rain' and 'Sleep Song'—set for soprano and small orchestra on the occasion of the Oxford Festival of 1926 and dedicated to Dorothy Silk and Sir Adrian Boult. They are chiefly interesting for their sensitive orchestral colouring. Of the choral music two of op. 36 are specially interesting; the first, a unison setting of Robert Greene's 'Sweet Obscurity', is another example of the supple melodic line in equal notes, and the second, Jonson's 'Hymn to Diana', makes distinguished play of gentle fifths over the piano's pedal-points. The unaccompanied four-part songs show Walker's fluid rhythm: 'Orpheus' and its haunting lilt and the late 'Sunset and evening star', op. 55, which moves through rich harmonies to a surprising last chord. 'Full fathom five', op. 34, for six unaccompanied sopranos, and anthems and a service written for Lady Margaret Hall are notable additions to works for female voices. A six-part choir matches the 'mellow touch of music' in Herrick's 'Soft Music', op. 48. The rich fabric is woven with masterly ease and the tranquil harmonies culminate in a wonderful cadence which does 'rather sigh than sound'.

But the climax of the choral music is the unaccompanied motet 'One generation passeth away'. It springs from a private grief but it uses terms of universal power. It resembles the Brahms 'Ernste Gesänge' in its consistently passionate pessimism, though in its harmony it is worlds away. It is most difficult of intonation.

The same impassioned sadness informs the unaccompanied 'Dirge in Woods' (Meredith), the last work, written in 1938. It is interesting to note that Walker had a setting of this poem in mind much earlier. In a 1915 examination paper for D.Mus. there is an unfinished piece in passionate style written on two staves and set for orchestration and completion. On the paper is a note—'This is the sketch for a possible opening of a choral setting of "Dirge in Woods".' In this last work there is sure mastery, showing the dignified fortitude of a mind which saw unbowed the heavens falling.

> And we drop like the fruits of the tree
> Even we
> Even so.

Of the later instrumental works the most substantial are the Fantasia-Variations on a Norfolk Folk-song, op. 45, and the Rhapsody and Fugue, op. 57, both written for piano duet (of all publicity-shunning mediums!). The Fantasia-Variations were arranged by the composer for orchestra with typical economy (double woodwind, two horns, a single trumpet, tympani, and strings) and in this version have achieved marked success. The tune used is 'Lovely Joan', collected at Acle by Vaughan Williams, and used by him on several occasions. Readers of Walker's essays will remember that he strongly resisted the prevailing tide of 'folkery' as far as art-music was concerned. He here pays some lip-service to modality and even shows that he is proficient at writing parallel common chords; but the persuasive charm of this quiet, even unobtrusive piece rests mainly in the subtle interplay of romantic harmonies; they culminate in an adagio section in three flats, but ambiguous in its tonality and built round a motto phrase which enshrines the name of the dedicatee. There is a sunset end in E major quite contrary to the pure Dorian of the tune; for Walker his own musical thought came first, and here it is especially beautiful.

The Rhapsody and Fugue is a piano duet, big music full of kaleidoscopic changes of colour and harmony. It is treated as an entirely different medium from the piano solo; there is a minimum of doubling and the part-writing is always lively without making the texture tediously thick. The Rhapsody is full of romantic fancy with Fauréan harmonic surprises, and the Fugue is a vigorous piece of sonorous rhetoric.

A third extended work is 'Variations on a theme of Joachim' for violin and piano, op. 40. It is a difficult work to assess. At first glance some parts, particularly the first variation[1] and the extremely difficult fifth variation with the triple-stopping, seem merely formal, and a superficial performance will but confirm this impression. But when the underlying meaning of the work is realized (its technical difficulty makes this far from easy), it is found deeply satisfying. Its many incidental felicities, and the beauty of Joachim's theme, will not be in dispute.

The later piano music is all on a small scale; much of it is composed on friends' initials and motto themes but from this apparently unpromising material are derived miniatures which become more significant with intimacy. Special mention should be made of the first of the Dedications, op. 42, the best example of this genre and a piece of surprising depth and power.

The three Fughettas, op. 49, are astonishing works. There is here a deliberate choice, such as made by some eighteenth-century composers, of angular themes of shifting tonality. This form of art is always a stimulus to a composer's technique. The second fughetta is especially sombre and deep and hints at harmonic abysses like those in Bach's three-part invention in F minor; the third is a 'sempre pianissimo' of great subtlety requiring a very considerable technique.

If the organ were more discerningly played and listened

[1] It was the composer's wish that in those phrases where the triplets are wholly above the sustained E, the E should be stopped on the A string, not open. In the fifth variation he wished the chords to be played with alternate bows, not successive down-bows.

to, there would be little doubt that the Preludes on the Lady Margaret Hall Hymn Tunes would have won wider recognition. The tunes themselves are notable for their flexible lines of equal notes, their leaping contours and their chaste, yet often unexpected, harmony. The Preludes are outstanding amongst twentieth-century organ music in combining exceptional musical worth with successful writing in a difficult medium. The majority of the preludes are quietly introspective, but two of them, 'Norham' and 'Windy Peak', move with splendid *élan*. The harmony is throughout in Walker's most original and powerful vein.

Most of Walker's unpublished work is chamber music in large forms. Three works are outstanding and need publication. They are the Variations for viola and piano (1908), the remarkably fine Variations for one-handed pianist, clarinet, and string trio (1933), and a breathlessly vivacious setting for high voice and piano of Henley's 'The Wind on the Wold' (1902).

Walker was also concerned with arrangements and editing. An idealist venture of Joseph Williams at the beginning of the century was the issue of volumes of selected arias from the church cantatas of Bach and the operas of Handel. Walker was the editor and set an impeccable standard. His sense of musical style made his task far harder than a less knowledgeable editor might have found it, for he was impelled to go to immense pains in ensuring that every significant detail had its logical place. Unfortunately the public did not respond and Walker's industry in this direction was not used again. There are two interesting items from the short list of arrangements for piano, one a setting of a delightful song, 'The Brooklet', by Edward Loder (who is highly praised in the *History of Music in England*), and the other an arrangement, which benefits from the change of medium, of the Allegro Assai from Mendelssohn's String Quartet in F minor, op. 80. In the essay on Mendelssohn in *Free Thought and the Musician* Walker refers to this scherzo as 'Half a dozen seldom-heard pages, not at all effective for their medium: but startling in their dark power and passion, and perhaps the first heralding of a man greater than the great youth we know.'

Works by Ernest Walker

PUBLISHED WORKS

NOTE. The date of publication is given: where this differs considerably from the date of composition the latter is also given.

Opus	Description	Publisher
1	Six Songs, medium voice and Pianoforte	Joseph Williams 1892
	a. Full fathom five (Shakespeare)	
	b. It was a lover and his lass (Shakespeare)	
	c. When icicles hang by the wall (Shakespeare)	
	d. Frühlingsglaube (Uhland) ⎫	
	e. Frühlingsruhe (Uhland) ⎬ English translation by the composer	
	f. Frühlingsfeier (Uhland) ⎭	
2	Six Two-part Songs, SS (or SA) and Pianoforte	do.
	a. To Daffodils (Herrick)	
	b. To Blossoms (Herrick)	
	c. Under the greenwood tree (Shakespeare)	
	d. Come unto these yellow sands (Shakespeare)	
	e. Lo, here the gentle lark (Shakespeare)	
	f. Music, when soft voices die (Shelley)	
3	Six Songs, voice and Pianoforte	do. 1893
	a. Orpheus with his lute (Shakespeare)	
	b. Phillis the fair (Burns)	
	c. What does little birdie say (Tennyson)	
	d. Die blauen Frühlingsaugen (Heine) ⎫ English transla-	
	e. Es liegt der heisse Sommer (Heine) ⎬ tion by the composer	
	f. Geheimnis (Karl Candidus) ⎭	
4	Variations on a Norwegian air, for Pianoforte *Dedicated to Fanny Davies*	do. 1894
5	Romance and Capriccio, for Pianoforte	do. 1895
6	Ballade for Violin and Pianoforte	do. 1896

Opus	Description	Publisher

7   Six Two-part Songs, SS (or SA) and Pianoforte   Joseph Williams
(Words from Blake's *Songs of Innocence*)   1897

     a. The Shepherd
     b. The Echoing Green
     c. A Cradle Song
     d. Night
     e. Nurse's Song
     f. Laughing Song

8   Sonata in A minor for Violin and Pianoforte   do. 1898
     Dedicated to Cecilia Gates   (composed 1895)

9   Romance in B flat for Viola (or Clarinet) and Piano-
     forte   do. 1898

10   Five Songs, words from 'England's Helicon' (1600) for
     4 solo voices (SATB) and Pianoforte (with Ger-
     man translation by Alexander Kastner)   do. 1900
     Dedicated to A. Foxton-Ferguson

     a. The Shepherd's Consort (out of M. Morley's
        Madrigals)
     b. Damelus' song to his Diaphenia (H. C.)
     c. Love the only price of love (Ignoto)
     d. Wodenfride's song in praise of Amargana
        (W. H.)
     e. A sweet Pastoral (N. Breton)

11, No. 1. Ballade for 'Cello and Pianoforte   do. 1900
     Dedicated to W. E. Whitehouse

11, No. 2. Adagio in E flat for 'Cello (or French Horn)
     and Pianoforte
     Dedicated to Paul Ludwig

12   Six Songs, low voice and Pianoforte   Acott & Williams
     a. Dream Land (Christina Rossetti)   undated
        Dedicated to Muriel Foster
     b. Wenn einstmals mir das Alter naht (Olga von
        Gerstfeldt) (trans. by the composer)
        Dedicated to Olga von Gerstfeldt
     c. The splendour falls on castle walls (Tennyson)
     d. Some asked me where the rubies grew (Herrick)
     e. Night-Piece (Herrick)
     f. Anacreontic Ode (Fill me, boy, as deep a
        draught—Thomas Moore)

Opus	Description	Publisher
13	Hymn to Dionysus for Chorus (SATB) and Orch. (Words from a chorus in Euripides' *Bacchae*, trans. Gilbert Murray) *Dedicated to H. P. Allen*	Novello, vocal score, 1906
14	Ode to a Nightingale (Keats) for Baritone solo, SATB chorus, and orchestra with concertante Clarinet	do. 1908
15	Anacreontic Ode for Baritone and Pianoforte (I care not for the idle state—Thomas Moore)	Joseph Williams 1890
16	Two Anthems for male voices and organ *Dedicated to Walter Parratt*	Paxton, 1899
	a. I will lift up mine eyes also issued for SSA	Revised and re-issued by Novello, 1947
	b. Lord, Thou hast been our Refuge also for SATB	
17	Six Three-part Songs, for SSA and Pianoforte	Joseph Williams
	1. Sister awake! (Anon., From an Elizabethan song-book) 1901	
	2. Hark, hark, the lark (Shakespeare) (unaccompanied) 1903 *Dedicated to Ruth, Margery, and Phyllis Eyre*	
	3. Roses, their sharp spines being gone (Fletcher) 1903 *Dedicated to the Singing Class at the Clergy Daughters' School, Casterton*	
	4. Song of Proserpine (Shelley) 1905	
	5. Say, dainty dames (Weelkes' *Ballets and Madrigals*, 1598) 1907 *Dedicated to Ruth, Margery, and Phyllis Eyre*	
	6. Urchins and Elves (Ravenscroft) 1908	
18	Song with Pianoforte: Corinna's going a-maying (Herrick) *Dedicated to Plunket Greene*	Boosey, 1902
19	Two Songs with Pianoforte 1. Stars of the summer night (Longfellow) *Dedicated to Francis Harford*	Willcocks, Berners St., 1903
	2. The Three Fishers (Kingsley)	

Opus	Description	Publisher
20	Minuet and Trio for two Violins and Pianoforte *Dedicated to the Violin Class, Sydenham High School for Girls*	Vincent Music Co., Berners St., 1903
21	Song with Pianoforte: Bluebells from the Clearings (W. E. Henley) (Charles Phillips Competition Prize)	Elkin, 1904
22	Intermezzo for Strings (two Clarinets *ad lib.*) and Pianoforte *Dedicated to the Orchestra of the Sydenham High School for Girls*	Vincent, 1906
23	Prelude and Fugue in D, for Organ *Dedicated to Basil Harwood*	Stainer & Bell 1908
24	Four-part Song (SATB unaccompanied) The splendour falls on castle walls (Tennyson)	do.
25	Three-part Song for SSA and Pianoforte The World's Wanderers (Shelley)	do.
26	Four-part Song, for TTBB unaccompanied Liberty (Shelley)	do.
27	Three Songs with Pianoforte 1. Hey Nonny No! (Elizabethan MS.) 2. In the spring twilight (Sydney Dobell) 3. Snowdrops (Sydney Dobell)	do. 1909
28	Song with Pianoforte Come into the garden, Maud (Tennyson)	do. 1911
29	Sonata in C for Viola and Pianoforte	Schott, 1912 (composed 1897)
30	Three Part-songs for SSA unaccompanied 1. To Music (Herrick) 1912 2. Epitaph upon a Virgin (Herrick) 1914 3. Upon a child that died (Herrick) 1914	Joseph Williams
31	Song for SSA and Pianoforte In Pride of May (words from an Elizabethan song-book)	Curwen, 1914

Opus	Description	Publisher
32	Fantasia for String Quartet in D	Fischer, New York, 1923 Novello, 1947 (composed 1905)
33	Part-song for SATB unaccompanied Orpheus with his lute (Shakespeare)	Stainer & Bell 1922
34	Song for six soprano voices, unaccompanied Full fathom five (Shakespeare)	do.
35	Incidental music for Euripides' *Rhesus*. In Greek. Male voices, unison and two-part	Oxford University Dramatic Society 1923
36	Five Songs	O.U.P. 1924

36.
1. Sweet Obscurity (Robert Greene) for unison voices and Pianoforte
2. Hymn to Diana (Ben Jonson) for three voices and Pianoforte
3. A Hawk's up, for a Hunt's up (Ravenscroft) for two voices and Pianoforte
4. Sleep (Beaumont and Fletcher) for two voices and Pianoforte
5. To an Autumn Rose (Mary Scott) for two voices and Pianoforte

37	Prelude in E flat for Pianoforte (Used for Variations in op. 44) *Dedicated to I.M.C.*	O.U.P. 1925 (composed 1904)
38	Songs with small orchestra (or Pianoforte) *Dedicated to Dorothy Silk and Adrian Boult* 1. Summer Rain (Dobell) 2. Sleep Song (Dobell)	O.U.P. 1926
39	Six Duettinos for Pianoforte duet	do.
40	Variations on a Theme of Joachim for Violin and Pianoforte *Dedicated to Jelly d'Aranyi*	O.U.P. 1927 (composed 1918)
41	Sonata in F minor for 'Cello and Pianoforte	O.U.P. 1928 (composed 1914)
42	Three Dedications for Pianoforte *Dedicated to Mrs. C. S. Deneke, H. C. Deneke, and M. Deneke*	O.U.P. 1929

Opus	*Description*	*Publisher*

43 Easter Piece for Pianoforte — Augener, 1929
Dedicated to Margaret Deneke

44 Sonata in E flat for Violin and Pianoforte — O.U.P. 1930
Dedicated to Gabriele Wietrowetz (composed 1910)

45 Fantasia-Variations on a Norfolk Folk-song ('Lovely Joan') — O.U.P. 1930
For Pianoforte duet, and also scored for orchestra by the composer.
Dedicated to Margaret Deneke

46 Four Miniatures for Pianoforte — O.U.P. 1931
Dedicated to Mrs. C. S. Deneke, for her and hers
  1. Ground
  2. Scherzetto (for a small dog)
  3. Canon
  4. Ostinato

47 Study for the left hand (Pianoforte) — Augener, 1931 (composed 1901)

48 Song for SSATBB unaccompanied — O.U.P. 1931
Soft Music (Herrick)

49 Three Fughettas, for Pianoforte — O.U.P. 1932

50 Ten Preludes for Organ on the Lady Margaret Hall Hymn Tunes. (For details see op. 51) — Novello, 1932

51 The Lady Margaret Hall Hymn Tunes — do.
Dedicated to H. C. and M. Deneke
  1. Buckau—for Herbert's 'Discipline' (Throw away Thy rod)
  2. Norham—for Herbert's 'Praise' (King of Glory, King of Peace)
  3. Water Meadow—for C. Rossetti's 'A Better Resurrection' (I have no wit, no words, no tears)
  4. Cambridge Gate—for Blake's 'To Mercy, Pity, Peace and Love'
  5. Warwick Haven—for Francis Quarles's 'Thou art my life'
  6. Overstrand—for Fletcher's 'Drop, drop, slow tears'
  7. Windy Peak—for Vaughan's 'Nativity' (Awake, glad heart)

Opus	Description	Publisher
	8. Letmathe—for Vaughan's 'Peace' (My soul, there is a country)	Novello, 1932
	9. Gunfield—for Vaughan's 'Cheerfulness' (Lord, with what courage and delight)	
	10. Denmark Hill—for Sidney's 'O Lord, in me there lieth nought'	
52	Motet for SSA unaccompanied The earth is the Lord's (also arranged for TBB) *Dedicated to the Choirmaster and Choir of Lady Margaret Hall, Oxford*	Novello, 1933
53	West African Fantasia for Pianoforte duet	O.U.P. 1933
54	Christmas Piece for Pianoforte *Dedicated to C. S. D., H. C. D., and M. D.*	Augener, 1933
55	Choral Song, for SATB unaccompanied Sunset and evening star (Tennyson)	O.U.P. 1934 (composed 1932)
56	Motet for SATB unaccompanied One generation passeth away (Ecclesiastes)	O.U.P. 1934
57	Rhapsody and Fugue for Pianoforte duet	O.U.P. 1934 (composed 1932)
58	Motet for SSA (unaccompanied or with *ad lib.* Pianoforte or Organ part) Hearken to me, ye that follow after righteousness (Isaiah) *Dedicated to the Choirmaster and Choir of Lady Margaret Hall, Oxford*	Stainer & Bell 1934
59	Londonderry Air, arranged for Violin and Pianoforte	O.U.P. 1935
60	A Waltz Suite for two Pianofortes	do.
61	Prelude for the left hand (Pianoforte)	Augener, 1935
62	Magnificat and Nunc Dimittis in D for Female Voices and Organ. (Mainly unison but some solos and some three-part writing) *Dedicated to the Choirmaster and Choir of Lady Margaret Hall, Oxford*	O.U.P. 1935
63	West African Fantasietta for Pianoforte solo	Augener, 1935

Opus	*Description*	*Publisher*
64	Canon for two equal voices and Pianoforte 'Ring out, wild bells' (Tennyson) *Dedicated to the Gunfield Choir*	Stainer & Bell 1937
65	Dirge in Woods (Meredith) for SATB unaccompanied	O.U.P. 1939

Published without Opus Number:
    Six two-part Solfeggi with Pianoforte accompaniment   Joseph Williams
                                                                                                            1894

EDITIONS AND ARRANGEMENTS

Ten Selected Arias from the Church Cantatas of J. S. Bach   Joseph Williams
                                                                                                                undated

Ten Selected Arias from the Operas of Handel   do.

Song: 'Muses, bring your garlands hither' from Purcell's
    'Elegy on the Death of Mr. John Playford'   O.U.P. 'Old
                                                                                            Master' Series
                                                                                            1927

'The Brooklet' (song by Edward Loder) arr. for Pianoforte   Augener, 1937
    solo

Londonderry Air (see op. 59)

Edition of Three Posthumous Pieces for Pianoforte by   Novello, 1947
    Mendelssohn
        1. 'Im Kahn'
        2. Song without words
        3. Canon

Allegro assai from Mendelssohn's String Quartet in F   do.
    minor, arr. for Pianoforte

UNPUBLISHED WORKS

1892 Lyrics for Strings

1892 Rhapsody in G minor for Pianoforte

1892 Psalm 130, 'De Profundis' for Solo Voices, Chorus, and Orchestra.

1893 Madrigal for five voices, 'Brown is my love'

1894 'From the Upland and the Sea' (William Morris) for Baritone, Pianoforte,
        and String Quartet
        Song, 'A Message' (G. H. F. Cookson)
        Song, 'Le Tsigane dans la lune' (Jean Lahor)

1895   Album Leaf for Pianoforte, No. 1
       Song, 'Why so pale and wan ?' (Suckling)

1896   Trio in C minor for Pianoforte, Violin, and 'Cello

1897   Mazurka for Pianoforte
       Concert Overture in F minor for Orchestra
       Stabat Mater for four solo voices, eight-part Chorus, and Orchestra

1898   Album Leaf for Pianoforte, No. 2
       Intermezzo in Tenths for Pianoforte
       Three songs (words by Olga von Gerstfeldt)

1899   Quartet in D for Pianoforte and Strings

1900   Quintet in B flat minor for Horn and Strings
       Newport School Song (words by L. W. P. Lewis)

1902   Song, 'The Wind on the Wold' (W. E. Henley)
       Three War Songs from Tennyson's 'The Princess'
       Two duets for Soprano and Baritone with Pianoforte
           1. My dearest love, since thou wilt go (Herrick)
           2. You that wont to my pipe's sound (words from an Elizabethan
              song-book)

1903   Song, 'Camilla fair' (words from an Elizabethan song-book)

1904   Duets for Contralto and Tenor (words by Heine)
       Seven short pieces for Pianoforte ('The days of the week')
           (No. 1 published as op. 37)
       Romance and Caprice for Violin and Pianoforte
       Cadenzas to Mozart's Pianoforte Concerto in D minor, K. 466

1905   Quintet in A for Pianoforte and Strings

1907   Variations on an original theme, for Viola and Pianoforte

1909   Song 'To Althea' (Lovelace)
       For the album of the Lovelace Club, Worcester College, Oxford

1910   Quartet in C minor for Piano and Strings
       Choral Lyric: 'Neptune's Empire' (Campion) for Chorus and Orchestra

1911   Ground for Strings (for Mrs. Molyneux and the Oxford High School
       for Girls Orchestra)

1913   Variations on an original theme for Pianoforte (left hand), Clarinet,
       Violin, Viola, and 'Cello (for Paul Wittgenstein)

1915   Cadenzas to Beethoven's Pianoforte concerto in C minor

1935   Cadenzas to Mozart's Pianoforte Concerti
           1. B flat K. 456
           2. C major K. 467
           3. A major K. 488

1937   Song with Pianoforte accompaniment from Schiller's 'Wilhelm Tell'

Index

PRINTED IN GREAT BRITAIN
AT THE UNIVERSITY PRESS, OXFORD
BY CHARLES BATEY, PRINTER TO THE UNIVERSITY